ISBN 978-0-259-25024-1
PIBN 10129323

1 MONTH OF
FREE
READING

at
www.ForgottenBooks.com

By purchasing this book you are eligible for one month membership to ForgottenBooks.com, giving you unlimited access to our entire collection of over 700,000 titles via our web site and mobile apps.

To claim your free month visit:

www.forgottenbooks.com/free129323

English
Français
Deutsche
Italiano
Español
Português

www.forgottenbooks.com

Mythology Photography **Fiction**
Fishing Christianity **Art** Cooking
Essays Buddhism Freemasonry
Medicine **Biology** Music **Ancient**
Egypt Evolution Carpentry Physics
Dance Geology **Mathematics** Fitness
Shakespeare **Folklore** Yoga Marketing
Confidence Immortality Biographies
Poetry **Psychology** Witchcraft
Electronics Chemistry History **Law**
Accounting **Philosophy** Anthropology
Alchemy Drama Quantum Mechanics
Atheism Sexual Health **Ancient History**
Entrepreneurship Languages Sport
Paleontology Needlework Islam
Metaphysics Investment Archaeology
Parenting Statistics Criminology
Motivational

LETTERS

—OF—

Gov. Benjamin Franklin Perry

—TO—

HIS WIFE.

" This was the noblest Roman of them all."

" She was his life;
The ocean to the river of his thoughts
Which terminated all."

SECOND SERIES.

GREENVILLE, S. C.:
SHANNON & CO., PRINTERS,
1890.

DEDICATED

TO OUR CHILDREN AND GRANDCHILDREN

WITH THE PRAYER THAT THEY

MAY FOLLOW THE NOBLE EXAMPLE

OF THE PARENT

WHO LOVED THEM SO FONDLY.

"His immortal part with angels live."

SANS SOUCI, GREENVILE, S. C., DECEMBER 3, 1889.

Third Anniversary of Our Separation.

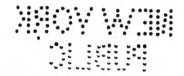

Truly yours R. H. Pruy

PREFACE.

"I think we had the chief all love's joys,
Only in knowing that we loved each other."

In Governor Perry's letters to his wife, he expressed the wish that his letters would be read with interest and profit in after years by his children, and in his Journal wrote that his Letters he hoped would be read one hundred years hence by his descendants. The paper on which he then wrote is crumbling and the ink fading. In order to carry out his wish his wife has had these letters printed to preserve them in durable form for our children. But inasmuch as they delineate the beautiful domestic character of their father, she is sure others will also read them with pleasure—these simple effusions of his heart—and appreciate Governor Perry's character more highly than ever. They will learn that his private virtues shown as brightly in his home as his public characteristics were resplendent before the world. They will realize that the devotion of his wife to his memory has not been shown in the least proportion to his deserts, and cannot be if she lives far beyond the allotted age of man. He merits all the love devotion, admiration and veneration a wife can give the noblest Husband, Father and Patriot that ever lived.

"My love shall be a crown of glory to thy brow,
And not a feeble hindrance in thy path."

NOTE.—Other letters will be published as opportunity offers.

INDEX.

"To that dauntless temper of his mind ;
He hath a wisdom that doth guide his valour
To act safely."

NASHVILLE, January 5, 1890.

MRS. B. F. PERRY,

DEAR MADAME: I acknowledge with many thanks the receipt of the "Letters of my Father to my Mother," and I assure you the reading of it has not only afforded pleasure, but confirmed the impression I have always entertained of the dignity, worth and excellence of human nature. There is certainly a spark of divinity in man. These letters were written with no view to publicity—the utterances were in the recesses of private confidence—and yet there is not a line that the author would be ashamed for the whole world to read. This fact shows *character*. You say I admire your husband—indeed I do. He was pure in private as in public life. He was no *actor*. To high intellectual qualities, literary acquirements, professional standing and fervid patriotism were added the gentle graces which mark the great man and *good* the Christian, of which these letters are an evidence. Again I thank you, and let me express my admiration for the devotion which you pay to the memory of so good a husband and so great a man.

I have looked through the pages of the "Southern Literary Messenger." I found a copy at the Vanderbilt University, and I am obliged to you; but the little poem of which I am in search was not printed in that magazine. I fear it is a lost treasure.

I have been ill for some days—scarcely able to hold the pen now—else I should sooner have replied.

Accept our congratulations of the season and best wishes for your health and happiness.

Very sincerely, your friend,
JOHN M. LEA.

NASHVILLE, Jan. 7th, 1890.

DEAR MADAME: I wrote to you the day before yesterday and have now the pleasure to acknowledge the receipt of your

Chief Justice John M. Lea. President of the Historical Society of
Tennessee, and Samuel C. Lea, of the Supreme Court, of
Tennessee.

letter of the 3d inst., which was received yesterday afternoon.
I have derived much pleasure from reading the letters, and
Mrs. Lea, who has the book now in her hands, is equally
charmed, and does me the honor to say they remind her of
the letters she received from me, only that my letters were not
so *full* of expressions of love. I tell her that she has forgotten what I did write. To some of my intimate friends, I shall
hand the volume for perusal, by whom, I know, their excellence
will be appreciated. The letters written after marriage show
the true, good, affectionate husband. I have not seen in any
letter a word or a sentence that required suppression.

The photograph and the picture of "Sans Souci" will ornament the walls of our house, alongside of those we love, and
I thank you for sending them to me, nor could you have sent
them to one who would prize them more highly.

I feel very much honored by the printing of my letter as an
appendix to the collection. The association of my name with
Governor Perry's is indeed an honor; and, madame, if you
feel kindly towards me because I express admiration for your
husband, I am glad. I believe that Governor Perry was an
unselfish patriot—a brave man who would have suffered mar-
tyrdom for what he believed to be the truth; who had the
courage to side in a minority of *one* when he thought he
was right—a good man and a great man—and, I am glad, that
in the declining years of my life, though I never saw him, I
made his acquaintance through his writings.

The typographichal errors do not blemish the text—and
faults are generally found in printing—not desirable, of course,
but no matter of great regret. In my letter, too—doubtless
owing to my handwriting—the word *diverse* should be sub-
stituted for *divine*, and I must ask you to make the correction
in any copies you have at your home.

My health has been feeble and the weather is most unfa-
vorable. This day is as warm as May. There has really been
no cold weather. The honey-suckle is in bloom, and the grass
is green. Christmas was shorn of the honor of frost and snow,
and there was heat enough without lighting the yule-log.

May Providence smile on you in age as it did in youth.

Very sincerely your friend,
JOHN M. LEA.

Elizabeth F. Perry.

LETTERS

OF

B. F. PERRY TO HIS WIFE.

COLUMBIA, S. C., THURSDAY EVENING.

MY DEAR LIZ: I have just purchased a *gold pen* with a diamond point, which it is said, will last fifty years without mending or altering, and I am disposed to write with it my first letter to you. It is something to receive a letter written with a gold pen, having a diamond point, and that letter too from a loving husband.

I was very much provoked and very uneasy yesterday evening. I did not know whether to be alarmed or angry, and so I concluded to indulge a little in both feelings. I went to the postoffice twice and could not get in. About eight o'clock in the night Col. Maybin sent, and reported to me on my return from the meeting of the Judiciary Committee, that there were no letters for me. It had been almost a week since I had heard from home. A great many things might have happened in that time. I assure you I was in a state of great uneasiness. The hope I still had that a letter there was for me in the postoffice. I went early this morning and sure enough there was, for which I thank you kindly. You can hardly conceive the pleasure and satisfaction it gave me—I found you were all well.

We have had most shocking weather for several days past. I had lost several of my cases in the Court of Appeals, and not receiving a letter from home made me feel bad enough, all put together. But the weather seems to have improved after receiving your letter and my feelings are very different. I have gained the most important case which I had and have two more yet unheard of, which I hope to gain also.

I was successful last night before the Judiciary Committee

in my case. The committee of the House reported a bill giving the property to the petitioners. I went before the Committee of the Senate this evening, but the case was postponed 'til to-morrow evening. If I am successful there I shall be ready to start home the first of next week. Unless Col. Barton wishes to employ me in some case before the Legislature. He came down to-night and said he wished to see me in the morning.

I have been very busy the two last days in examining students in Law and Equity. I was placed on both Committees by the Judges. There were very near fifty students admitted in the two Courts. Amongst them was your cousin Alston Hayne and Major Colcock—also, Stokes of Greenville, the son-in-law of Mr. Kilgore.

Young Hayne told me yesterday that your uncle Arthur's daughter, Fanny, was to be married that evening, in the country, at Col. Hayne's house. He said he was anxious to have gone to the wedding but could not.

I was in treaty for one of Holmes chairs when I received your letter informing me that your mother had got one for Anne. I stepped into Johnson's book store and saw one. It occurred to me immediately that it would suit Anne, and I was going to purchase it for her. It is certainly the finest chair for a sick person that could be found—the price of this one was $23.00. It must be a great convenience and comfort to Anna.

I have made no further purchases since I wrote you last, save the gold pen with which I am now writing, the price of which was $4.00, and if it will last me fifty years it will be the cheapest pen ever made. Professor Ellett has been writing with one for five years and it is a good pen yet—two or three others in this place have used one of them for three years. You see I write very well with it, and I have written very fast. It will make my handwriting plainer and more uniform and better.

I wish to see you and the children very much and am getting very impatient to leave here—yet I ought to stay if I have any notion of running for Solicitor. The election of

Judge is very doubtful—I am not able to say now who will be elected, nor even conjecture.

It is my intention to pay off all my debts as soon as I reach home. The sale of my bank stock was a fortunate one. The stock has already fallen to 48 cents in the dollar.

The bell now summons me to supper, at nine o'clock in the night, so I must conclude my letter. God bless you and the children, dear wife. B. F. PERRY.

NEWBERRY C. H., November 20. 1842.

MY DEAR LIZ: I have time only to write you a few lines whilst I am in the same room with Duncan, Ware, Townes and Choice.

We had quite a pleasant journey down here, but have had a most angry and stormy time since our arrival here. The Railroad Convention broke up in confusion. The Greenville and Laurens stockholders withdrew and severed their connection with the Company. The reason of this was that the road was located in Abbeville and Anderson instead of running through Laurens. The Greenville and Laurens subscribers are now relieved from the payment of their stock. We have had much debate and some angry discussion—none on my part though, some on the part of General Thompson and others.

We start in the morning to Columbia. Colonel Coleman, Poinsett, Blake and their families are at Hunt's and go down to-morrow or next day.

I took tea with Col. Fair. He lives in great style. I was at Chancellor Johnston's, who lives handsomely, and he invited me to tea, but I could not accept.

The Laurens people are outraged with Colonel Orr for his course on the railroad. I made two good speeches in the convention, and was highly complimented for them.

Edward has been standing by me, and says give his respects to you and tell his mother "howdy" and all the rest of the servants. He says that he is very much pleased with his journey, and has behaved himself well.

Choice is considerably hurt by his runaway scrape.

Tell Will I wish very much to have him with me, and I am sorry I did not bring him in the carriage. Kiss the children. Tell Will to write me.

I wrote you a long letter by Dr. Irvine. I sent you by Mr. Wells a beautiful present—a set of castors and a pair of candlesticks at $35. I have just been to a book auction and purchased a great many beautiful books, but can not get them to send to-night—some annuals and beautiful prints. I will send them the first opportunity. In great haste. God bless you. Write as often as possible. Yours, etc.

                                        B. F. PERRY.

COLUMBIA, November 25th, 1842.

MY DEAR LIZ: I have just finished dressing and taken my seat to write you a few lines before breakfast, as I do not expect to have time to write afterwards before the mail is closed. I hope you wrote me yesterday and will add a postscript for to day.

We reached Columbia yesterday evening, all safe, after a pleasant journey down, with the exception of an accident, which had like to have been a very serious affair. The second day after leaving Greenville, we were disappointed in getting lodgings at the house where we expected to stay, and had to drive two miles further in the dusk of the evening. I had taken a seat with Judge Earle and his boy was driving my horse and buggy. In passing through a drove of hogs, which had been to water, in the lane and in front of the house where we were going to stay, one of the hogs ran under the heels of one of Judge Earle's horses and frightened them. They ran up the hill and we thought their scare was over. But whilst enquiring about lodgings one of the horses commenced kicking, plunging, wheeling round, etc. The other horses were all behind and became alarmed also and manifested a disposition to join in the frolic. It was then quite dark. I sprung out of the Judge's buggy and ran to my horse's head and made Edward go to hold the judge's horses, one of which was kicking at a most terrible rate all the time. Colonel Cox unloosed his horses from the carriage just in time. In order to get my horse out of the way I drove through a gate, and I had scarcely got through when the Judge's buggy and horses and two or three men who were trying to hold his horses, made a dash at the place I had just left. Had I not been out of the way we should have had a general crash. After some time a half dozen men succeeded in getting the horses extricated from the carriages. But the frightened horse was not satisfied, but continued to kick, and came very near giving Sam Earle a blow which might have made another widow in Mrs. Harrison's family. Colonel Cox received a severe kick on his hand. Judge Earle came out safe. The carriage was considerably injured; the horse badly crippled. I thought at one time we should have a "general runaway." The next morning the Judge got a new horse and mended his carriage and we all came on safely.

We had some fine dinners on the road out of the provisions we carried with us. Judge Earle again praised the corn pound cake and ginger bread. It is so much more pleasant eating on the roadside than stopping at a house for dinner.

I hope you and the children are all doing well. I talked to Judge Earle so much about the pleasure we derive from a wife and children, that I believe he seriously determined to get married. He regretted his situation very much and said he had nothing but a dreary and gloomy future, full of unhappiness and misery.

I saw Colonel Martin last night. He says they are all well. I have not yet seen Mr. Hayne. There are ten or fifteen candidates for Secretary of State. I have never seen so much electioneering. I feel happy that I am not a member. The old members are all expressing to me great regret that I am not a member.

I have a room with Mr. Burt, but he has not yet arrived. In it there is a fine chest of drawers, locked. I supposed they were empty. I took out my bunch of keys to try to unlock them. I found a key and unlocked them, when behold—

instead of being empty, contained a *lady's wardrobe!* All the paraphanalia of a female's dress with a great many *et ceteras.* I was reminded of the story of *Blue Beard.* I had got into forbidden ground. I locked up the drawers and put the keys back in my pocket.   Yours truly,

                     B. F. PERRY.

COLUMBIA, December 1st, 1842.

MY DEAR LIZ: I was disappointed in writing to you yesterday as I intended doing. I was all day waiting in court for one of my cases to be taken up, and it was not till this morning. I have just finished the argument in that case and have left the court for the purpose of writing to you. I had the good fortune to try one of my cases last Tuesday. So I have, now, *two* disposed of and *six* more to argue, besides two in the Legislature. I shall be detained here eight or ten days yet.

In consequence of my rooming with Mr. Burt I cannot write you as conveniently as I could if I were alone. We have *two sets* of visitors to entertain in consequence of our being together.

Your letters were received this morning, and I need not speak of the pleasure they gave me. I read them both whilst with Sam Earle, and had the pleasure of telling him that Mrs. Earle was well, etc. Poor old George looks very natural and is working for Dr. Roach. I do not know what to say about your mother buying him. She must determine the matter for herself. You know my plan is not to purchase an old negro. Your mother can determine for herself and write me.

I have been tempted to purchase for Susan one of the sweetest little gold pencil-cases you ever saw. The price was seven dollars, but I got it for four and one-half; so I have paid $4.50, and will present the gold pencil case to her. It is substantial, and will look prettier and last longer than a silver one. It was so beautiful I could not resist the temptation of buying it, and making it a present. If you wish me

I will get you one like it. It has a ring to hang to a chain and is beautifully carved.

I have seen a horse, and think of buying it for Will. The price is $14.00. I cannot get it for less, but the difficulty will be in getting it home. I do not think of going to Augusta now, as I can arrange the business I have there by sending the money by Ben Yancey, who is now here and is in Augusta every day when at home. By the by, Ben Yancey says he has the prettiest little specimen of female beauty he ever saw. I doubted that I had not a prettier in little Anna. Yancey made a very good speech the other day in the Court of Appeals.

I am more and more pleased at not being in the Legislature, and would not take a seat there now for several hundred dollars. I have seen so much intriguing and electioneering this session that I am utterly disgusted with politics.

Colonel Preston has resigned, and Mr. Calhoun intends doing so. The Legislature will have two Senators to elect. Great exertions are making by the Rhetts to have Barnwell Rhett elected. The friends of Judge Huger will perhaps put him in nomination. Gevernor Richardson, Judge O'Neal, Colonel McWillie, are all spoken of. McDuffie will be the successor of Colonel Preston. I saw Col. Preston this morning. He looks remarkably well and has returned to the Bar. Judge Butler came to see me the other night and enquired after all of you very kindly. In giving the Judges my Briefs I gave him one that you had endorsed last fall. He said he would keep it on account of the writing. Albert Rhett came twice to see Burt and myself and enquired after all of you very kindly.

Mr. Hayne tells me he has a box for your mother, but has not yet sent it to me; nor have I sent the box of Susan to him. Mrs. Taylor's health is much better.

I am very glad to hear that the children and servants are behaving well, and am sorry to hear of Anne's bad health again. I hope she will get better. I saw Colonel Keith, who came to my room electioneering. He has Mrs. Keith with him. Her health is bad. He has been elected and will return to town. He enquired after all of you; how many children, etc. He looks badly. I went down to the State House this morning to meet the Bible convention, but it did not meet. Kiss the children and give my love to your mother, etc.   Most Affectionately,

B. F. PERRY

COLUMBIA, S. C., December 5th, 1842.

MY DEAR LIZ: Your letter was handed me last night and Mr. Earle came up to know what the news was from home, and to my surprise, had not heard from his better half since he had left Greenville. I was much pleased to hear that you were all doing pretty well. I begin to feel anxious to see you and the children. How I sould like to take them in my arms and hear their prattle! I will endeavor to be at home the first of next week.

I have just returned from the college commencement to write you. I saw there a great display of beauty and fashion, but did not stay long to admire it—not more than three minutes.

This morning I started with your letter in my hand to shop. I found all the articles you desired and have made the purchases. Tell Will I have bought him a most beautiful pony, with a beautiful saddle and bridle, long tail and mane, high head, price $16.00. Colonel Johnson's waggon will be down here next week, and will carry the horse up for nothing. It is really a most beautiful *hobby horse*, and Will can ride on it most gloriously.

Mr. Hayne sent me two bundles for your mother, and I gave him the box which I brought down, or rather I sent it to Mrs. Taylor. I have not yet seen Taylor or any of his family.

I hope you received the gold pencil and letter sent you by Colonel Townes. I would write to you oftener than I do, but really I have no chance. Our room is continually filled with company. I am now writing whilst Burt and Colonel Davie and Reed are talking about all sorts of things, and I have to join in the conversation every now and then.

There is great excitement in regard to the election of United States Senator. Judge Huger and Barnwell Rhett and Colonel Davie are candidates. I think Judge Huger will be elected. I hope he will, and shall do all I can to insure his elction.

I saw Mr. Pendleton this morning. He gave me the magnolia and a beautiful print of Charleston. You will, however, see the print, as it will come with the magnolia.

I am very much complimented by all who see me on account of my good looks. I am told that I have improved astonishingly in personal appearance. They all say that I have fattened, look younger, etc. Laurens District will be added to Greenvilie and Pendleton as a congressional district, and Mr. Young declares I must be the candidate, but fortune will not permit me.

I have gained one of my cases in court and *tried* one in the Legislature—the road case in court. Spriggs and Barton's is in the Legislature, but they have not yet decided on it.

I have received a letter from W. Gilmore Simms. He says it is well that he was tempered down to a Benedict before he met with Anne, or he should have lost his heart, and says he will be very happy if his prescription of cold water could be of service to her.

I must conclude, my dear wife, as I am writing without thinking; there is so much talk going on. Kiss the children.
Yours truly,
B. F. Perry

Columbia, S. C.

My Dear Liz: I sent you this morning by Colonel Barton and Mr. Spriggs, one box, one trunk and one bundle. They will be delivered to you Saturday sometime in the day by Colonel Barton. Be kind and polite to him, for he is a good friend of mine, and has very kindly offered to carry anything I desired to send you.

The trunk will contain a bundle from Mr. Hayne, Will's silver cup, which I carried down with me, Sears' Bible and

Pictorial Illustrations, (three volumes) which I send as a present to my dear wife, and which you will value, both for the gift and *giver*. The trunk also contains three volumes of Harpers Family Library, also Rowland's Macassar Oil and two other boxes or vials. The contents of the box are unknown to me. Mr. B. Carrol told me last night that Miss Seabrook had sent it by him. I sent for it this morning to send by Colonel Barton.

I hope to hear from you this evening, as I am beginning to be very restless and anxious to see you and the children. I trust, however, you are all doing well.

I argued Mr. McBee's case yesterday, and was more than two hours reading my argument in the Court of Errors. After I had concluded Mr. Burt got up to speak on the same side, and Chancellor Job Johnston said he did not wish to hear any further argument on my side, and went out of court. Judge Richardson did the same. This was quite a compliment to my speech. Mr. Burt addressed the other Judges for about an hour, and made a capital argument. You may tell Mr. McBee that I have very little doubt of our success. Judges Evans and Richardson are with us, so is Chancellor Job Johnston; and Judge Butler, I think, has been brought over by Burt's and my argument. He gave me a favorable intimation this morning. Judges Earle and Wardlaw would not try the case. Judge Harper is absent. Dunkin and David Johnson will decide the case. Judge O'Neall is against me.

I have just left the Court House after axamining the law students. My student, Reed, was admitted, and all the others except one.

The election of Senator is exciting great interest. I think Judge Huger will be elected. Barnwell Rhett and Colonel Pickens and Colonel Davie are also candidates. Judge Butler is not, and is provoked at the notice of him in the *Mercury*.

I have not yet bought the bells, nor the gold pencil case for you. You must write me on that subject.

I was told by Mr. Middleton last night that it was understood that Colonel Frost and myself were candidates for the next vacancy on the Bench. I assured him that it was a mistake so far as I was concerned.

Tell Will his horse will reach home in the course of two weeks. I hope to be at home myself sooner than that. This matter of Spriggs, and Colonel Barton's will give me some trouble in the Legislature. Colonel Barton has offered me a fee of $500 if I can get the lease of the State Road for him for five years, and $1,000 if I can get it for ten years. I will try.

In haste. Yours truly. Kiss the dear little children for me, and give my love to your mother and sisters.

Affectionately, B. F. PERRY.

COLUMBIA, S. C.

MY DEAR LIZ: I have just heard of the death of my father. Mr. Duncan informed me that Mrs. Foster had just returned from Tugaloo and brought the intelligence. It was a great shock to me, and although he was very old, yet it grieved me much to think I had not seen him before his death. When I last saw him in the summer, little did I think it was to be a final parting between us in this world. You know it was our intention to have visited them last fall. How sorry I am we did not do so! It would have been a great consolation to me now if we had done so, and had shown him our two little children, one of whom he never saw. My father possessed many sterling virtues, which I would not have had him to exchange for all the hollow heartedness and pomp of wealth and fame. He possessed a kind heart and a stern, unbending integrity of character, which would do honor to anyone. There never lived a more honest or just man. I am sure he never did an intentional injury to anyone, and I believe he did all the good to his fellowmen which lay in his power. I am sure that there is nothing in his long life to exclude him from happiness in another world.

I am very anxious to be at home once more and see you and the dear little children. I shall finish the last of my business on Monday in the Legislature. I have already disposed of my

business in court, and if God spares me, I shall leave here on
Tuesday morning. You may expect me at home on Thursday
evening, unless the weather should be so bad as to prevent
my travelling. It is now raining, and I am afraid it will not
clear off before Tuesday.

To morrow morning I shall hear all about my cases, and I
will write again.

I shall be at home Thursday evening; but this letter will
reach you one day sooner. My cases are not yet all decided;
the case of Cauble is not. I saw Judge Earle this morning,
who told me all about them. I have gained Mr. McBee's case,
and you may send him word to that effect.

I went to see judge Huger last night. He looks very well.
Governor Hammond was inagurated on Saturday. There
was a great crowd at the Inauguration. Mr. Burt has gone
home, and I am now alone in my room. I hope Judge Huger
will be elected Senator. I have purchased four bells, cranks,
pullies, wire, etc., etc., for hanging them, and they cost
$5.87. I have got the spoon marked for Anna, and my
sleeve buttons also. I will get a Prayer Book.   Your
affectionate husband,

B. F. PERRY.

PICKENS C. H.

MY DEAR LIZ: I write you by Mr. Taylor, our Sheriff,
merely to say that it is altogether uncertain when I shall be
able to return. The court may sit all the week. There is
not, however, much business—that is, *paying* business. I have
received $55.00 in cash.

I saw Lee and delivered your package. Foster is here and
foreman of the grand jury. They are all well. The Verners
are not here. Old Mr. Verner is very sick.

I hope you and the children are doing well. Tell Reuben
he must go on plowing as fast as he can. Let him get peas
and plant with the corn. Yours truly and sincerely.

B. F. PERRY.

LAURENS C. H., October 10th, 1843.

MY DEAR LIZ: It is now late in the night, and I hope that you, Miss Pamela, and the children, (dear *little* creatures,) all of you, are sweetly reposing in the arms of that *leaden eyed deity,* of whose embraces no husband, or lover is ever jealous, no matter how much they may be sought for and enjoyed. I have just finished looking over Mr. Speer's forthcoming volume of Reports, which contain several of my *able* and *learned* arguments in the Court of Appeals. This, you may be certain, afforded me no little gratification; and I hope you will not feel your noble self slighted when I tell you that for the time being you and the children were out of my thoughts; but this letter is an evidence of the quickness with which you were recalled.

The fore part of the evening I spent in conversation with Judge Butler. He possesses his usual flow of spirit, wit and humor. I love him much. The Judge is a noble hearted fellow, liberal, generous, high minded and honorable.

We have very few lawyers in attendance on this court. Burt is at Edgefield, Henry has gone to Union, General Caldwell to Sumter, General Whitner heard of the extreme illness of his brother-in-law, Dr. Harrison, last night, and returned post haste to Anderson, leaving me the Solicitor's duties to perform, which will consist principally in prosecuting some pugilists for an affray and assault and battery. This may detain me here longer than I intended to stay. It is probable that I may not be at home till Friday night.

Tell Miss Pamela that I have not had the pleasure of meeting either her father or brother at this court, and I am afraid it will be out of my power to visit Rosemont during my stay here, than which nothing would give me greater pleasure. The letter which she intrusted to my care, was deposited in the postoffice early Monday morning, and I have no doubt has gone safely.

I know you are fond of news, like all of Mother Eve's daughters, and I therefore give you an item which I have just heard from Judge Butler. It is rumored that Colonel Pickens is going to be married to Colonel John E. Colhoun's daughter, about sixteen or seventeen years old! Dr. Laborde too is about taking to himself another wife, Miss Carroll, his sister-in-law! How lucky these old widowers are! How easily they fool the young girls! And how complimentary to the memory of their departed wives! They have found the married state one of so much happiness that they cannot exist out of it!

If you see Mrs. Coleman tell her that the Colonel's law suit is not yet tried. I promised to write him by this mail if it had been tried. Both Young and myself are in good spirits in regard to the case. It is one of considerable importance to Colonel Coleman.

I hope you and Miss Pamela are keeping house finely with the help of the children and servants to keep you straight. When did you have your company? You have had fine evenings for company. The weather is delightful, and I hope you have had no further visitations from the toothache—and that Miss Pamela has entirely forgotten that there is any such thing as a nervous disease at all, or such medicine as calomel. And I hope the children, little Will, Anna and Frank, have all forgotten how to cry!! In all these good wishes I am sure you will all join me most heartily.

I am not so well myself as I was when I left home. This I say in truth and in compliment to you and the dinner which your kindness provided me with on the road. I ate too much. I stopped on the road and had quite a *social meal* with *my horse!* He is indeed a civilized brute, and possesses a much more refined taste than most *Kentuckians*. He ate several of the rolls, a large portion of the fruit cake and smacked his mouth as if it was a most delicious morsel, much better than the food every day given him by his *worthless groom*. I offered him a piece of ham, but he turned up his nose at the gross and vulgar food and seemed to say that it should not touch his lips after your pound cake. I ate too much and have been starving myself ever since, which suits the Tavern here remarkably well. There ought to be professorships of cookery——

But I must now go to bed. I can imagine to myself the great stillness at home to-night, and your situation to-morrow evening when you receive this letter. Will and

Anna will have gone to bed—perhaps not yet asleep—talking to each other in the dark. Frank taking his supper—you and Miss Pamela seated around the lamp engaged in work. Is this a true picture? Good night, and God bless you.

Yours affectionately,
B. F. PERRY.

ANDERSON C. H., Oct. 24, 1843.

MY DEAR LIZ: I will write you a few lines to-night, as I expect Colonel Townes will leave for Greenville in the morning.

It is altogether uncertain when I shall be at home. We are now in the midst of a case of perjury, which excites considerable interest and will take the greater part of to-morrow. I think our defendant will be acquitted. His name is Clardy. You heard of the case some three or four weeks since.

I have been employed as assistant counsel in a case of slander. Our client is a very pretty young woman, who sues a neighbor woman for imputing to her a want of chastity. We expect to recover heavy damages. The appearance of the young woman will be much in her favour, I hope, with the Judge and jury. Almost every one would be more disposed to punish another quicker for slandering a pretty woman than an ugly one.

You need not be surprised if I bring home with me another servant—a man about 18 or 20 years old, honest and good looking, black colour—about the colour of 'Sinda. He is uncommonly smart—raised in North Carolina, sold for debt and the only negro owned by his master. His name is "Jim" —two Jims—what think you of the name? But you know we may distinguish by calling one "James." Price $700 in railroad stock. However, the bargain is not yet completed.

I have been very uneasy about you and the children ever since I left home. I hope, however, that the *grippe* has passed you by. Everybody here is unwell with it. Never heard of an influenza so general in my life. I wish you would write to me by return mail how you all are. I will get your letter Thursday morning. You can write a few lines after receiving this letter, before the mail closes.

Judge Butler showed me a letter he received on Monday from his little daughter. She is quite well and writes very well for a child of nine years old. The letter was only five lines.

I saw Mrs. Dr. Haynesworth and her son pass through here in the stage this morning, on their way to Greenville to see Mr. Elias Earle.

Judge Earle has resigned and requested Judge Butler to inform me of it. He asked Judge Butler who he thought should take his place. Judge Butler told me that he said he thought *I* would make a very good Judge. I replied that I thanked him, but should not be a candidate. I feel most flattered to be thought so well of by both Judge O'Neall and Judge Butler and I have no doubt Judge Earle would have agreed with them.

I shall endeavor to be at home on Friday night, if not sooner. If Colonel Cox should send to take away Exception, to winter her, tell the boy I have changed my mind and will keep her at home. I am afraid some accident may happen to her if sent off.

In great haste, as I have to prepare to-night for my speech to-morrow. Kiss the little children for me. I do hope they have no more of the grippe. I am pretty well myself. I hope the servants are all doing well, especially 'Sinda. Tell her I have seen "*Aunt Emily*," and that she made inquiry after her.

Good night, my dear Liz. God bless you and protect you —you and the children.

Yours truly, etc.,

B. F. PERRY.

ANDERSON C. H., Friday Morning.

MY DEAR LIZ: I have risen this morning before daylight, in order to write you a few lines by Messrs. Walker and Choice. I am now writing by candle light.

Your letter was received yesterday, about 12 o'clock, whilst

I was engaged in the trial of my slander case. It relieved me very much. I was afraid that you or the children might be unwell with the *grippe.* I hope the servants are better.

I shall endeavor to get home to-morrow evening. We were all day yesterday trying the case of slander which I mentioned in my other letter. The jury did not return till nine o'clock in the night. They gave the young lady $875, which with the costs, is just as much as the defendant is worth. It will entirely ruin him. I made a good speech, say the judge and lawyers. We were nearly two days trying the case of perjury, and my argument in that case has been much complimented. This has been a good court for me and I have done well. I begin to feel as if I were now in a way to do well and acquire a reputation as a lawyer.

I have taken the boy Jim on trial. He is now waiting on me, and I have never seen a more faithful servant. He is awkward and has never been accustomed to the duties of a body servant, but he is uncommonly intelligent and devoted to me. He is so extremely anxious to belong to me. He has more sense than half of the ignorant white people. I have no doubt he will make a valuable servant. I told him he must take Delia for a wife, which seemed to please him. He never has had a wife, and is eighteen or nineteen years old; weighs one hundred and forty pounds.

We have had rainy weather for a day or two and still appears cloudy. Judge Butler has been and is still unwell with a cold. I have escaped.

You informed me that Mrs. Cunningham was in Greenville. I suppose the weather has been so bad she has hardly gone yet. I am sorry to hear that Pamela is so unwell.

I have not heard from any of my mother's family.

You may expect to see me Saturday evening, and I assure you that I am becoming quite anxious to meet you and the children. It is a great pleasure—that of returning home to one's wife and children. Yours truly and sincerely,

B. F. Perry.

ANDERSON C. H., Wednesday Morning.

DEAR LIZ: I have barely time to write you that I will be at home to-morrow. I have been detained longer than I expected on account of the trial of Mr. Rodgers. His trial comes on this morning. If possible, I will go part of the way home this evening. I am very impatient to leave.

I have nothing at all to write, if I had time, but Mr. Choice is waiting for this scrawl. I hope you are doing well and that all matters are going on well.

My dear wife, yours in haste,
B. F. PERRY.

PICKENS C. H., Tuesday Morning.

MY DEAR LIZ: I will write you a line by Mr. Thompson, who says he is going to Greenville this morning.

I hope Will is not unwell from the medicine he took, but I always feel as if something might happen, when I am from home.

We have had fine weather and I hope you come on bravely with whitewashing and dusting carpets.

There is not much business in court, and I shall probably be at home on Thursday or Friday.

My horse did badly coming to this place; made me walk, and I led him up all the hills. He will not pull well in the buggy.

I must conclude, as persons have come in. God bless you. Kiss the children for me.   Yours, etc.,
B. F. PERRY.

ANDERSON C. H., Wednesday Morning.

MY DEAR LIZ: I have only time to write you a line by Colonel Townes, who has just informed me that he returns to Greenville to-day.

I do not know when I shall be at home, perhaps not till Friday or Saturday. There is not a great deal of business in court, but they get on slowly. Yesterday they were trying a Baptist preacher for disturbing a religious congregation at worship. He defends himself and is slow and tedious.

I hope you and the children are all well and doing well. I am in constant dread of the scarlet fever, but hope that as we have escaped so far we may entirely.

I have heard nothing from those fighting men worth stating. It is thought that Yancey and Alexander will not fight. Judge Earle is in Charleston on his way home, it is believed, as his trunks arrived there some time since.

When Jim has finished the oats, let him cut wood to haul.
In haste, yours, etc.,   B. F. PERRY.

LAURENS C. H., Tuesday Night.

MY DEAR LIZ: I intended to have written you a long letter this morning, but I have been so much engaged with my client, Dr. Teague, and his witnesses, that I have barely time to say to you that I shall not be at home till the last of the week.

I have been engaged in some very important cases here. One of them involves $40,000—as to the solidity of a will; the other is a case of importance, in both of which I shall get big *fees*, so you will not be sorry for my absence.

It is now eleven o'clock and I must bid you good-night.

John Cunningham and McGowan fight on Thursday. Alexander left here this evening to be present at the combat. It is probable Yancey and Alexander will not fight.
Yours, etc.,   B. F. PERRY.
P. S.: Kiss the children for me.

LAURENS C. H., Thursday Night.

MY DEAR LIZ: I am still here, and do not know when it will be possible for me to leave. We have just finished, after two whole days work, the case of Teague's will, and I am very sorry to say the case has been decided against me; but my client must ultimately gain the property, as we have appealed and there is another will.   Colonel Irby and Sullivan were against the will and Mr. Young and myself for it. For three days past I have been incessantly engaged in the case, either in the trial or in studying the case. It is one of great importance to the parties, and involves $40,000. It has been tried once before on the Circuit and in the Court of Appeals. We were all day to-day making speeches.

The other case in which I am engaged may not come up before Saturday and I may not be at home before Sunday. I hope, however, to get home by twelve o'clock Saturday, as I am to met Kirksey there at that time to file a bill in equity for him.

Whilst we were speaking two young men—Wright and Simpson—employed themselves in sketching the Judge and the counsel. Inclosed I send you two rude sketches which they made of me. They will do for you to laugh at. Judge Evans took the one they made of him and put it up carefully.

We have had dreadful weather all the week, and I am afraid Jim has not been able to sow oats. If not, I suppose you have had him whitewashing.

I hope you and the children are all well and doing well. I begin to wish very much to see you all. For two or three days past I have hardly had time to think about you. Last night I sat up till half past eleven o'clock, preparing my speech. I have to-night to make out the grounds of appeal, which will take me a long time. My speech is very highly complimented by the crowd.

If I had known that I should have been here so long I should have requested you to write me. It would give me great pleasure to hear from home.

Please send the enclosed letter to Lester in the morning.

Your affectionate husband,

B. F. PERRY.

LAURENS C. H., Friday Morning.

MY DEAR LIZ: I have time only to write you a line. I shall

be at home Sunday. My cases here have been postponed, and one of them, Dr. Anderson's, referred to a jury next fall.

I hope you will send a note to Mr. Rosmond about Jim cutting oats; Mr. Croft will send it up to his farm. Tell Reuben to commence the oats as soon as he finishes up the corn.

I had quite a pleasant ride down here with the Judge, and we stopped at a well and took our repast.

I hope the children are all well. I have nothing to write. In great haste. Yours affectionately,

B. F. Perry.

Laurens C. H., Wednesday.

My Dear Liz: I received your letter Tuesday morning and was much gratified to hear Frank was better. I am very anxious to hear again, and hope you will write me by the return stage. I shall not be able to return home before the last of the week. I have a slander case which detains me.

Yesterday we had a great railroad meeting and I made a long speech. General Thompson, Colonel Irby and Mr. Young also addressed the meeting. The people are beginning to feel an interest in the road.

Last night I went with Judge Evans to the Episcopal Fair. The company was small and the variety of articles for sale not great. I saw Mr. and Mrs. Arthur there, also Mr. Simpson and his lady.

Mr. Cunningham is here on the jury and will be here all the week. His family are still at Mr. Yancey's. He is going to send a message to Simms and seems a good deal excited.

We have another railroad meeting to-day. I am anxious to hear from the Greenville elections. You must take good care of Frank and get him well before I return.

In great haste, Yours truly and sincerely,

B. F. Perry.

My Dear Liz: I have only time to say that I am well and I hope you and the children are. I feel some uneasiness about you; but your message by General Thompson was that you were a great deal better. I hope to find you entirely well.

I do not know when I shall get off; perhaps to-morrow and perhaps not till Sunday morning. There is a good deal of business and I have a fair share. We are now trying a most important case. The jury have gone out.

I hope you are getting on well with the servants. I suppose Susan stays with you.

Do kiss the children for me. I wish I had Will with me.

General Thompson is just starting and I did not know he was going so soon. In haste, yours truly,

Thursday, 10 o'clock.   B. F. PERRY.

PICKENS C. H., Tuesday Night.

MY DEAR LIZ: It is uncertain when I shall be able to leave here; not before the last of the week, and perhaps Sunday.

We are now in the midst of Kirksey's case, and the result is doubtful. If I gain it he gives me $200 more. General Thompson and myself are on oue side, General Whitner and Mr. Young on the other. If I succeed in Reed's case I am to get an additional fee of part of the verdict. I hope to recover several hundred dollars, and perhaps thousands.

My brother Foster is here as foreman of the grand jury. He tells me that mother has lost a young negro woman and that Lucy is not expected to live; the same disease that proved fatal to Josiah's family. It is also in Shelor's family. Josiah is quite well again, but not here. I saw Verner, and Lee, the brother of Mrs. Duboc. They are all well.

I hope you and the children are all well and that you have had no trouble with the servants. It is better to pass over their idleness and impudence than to always keep yourself in "hot water" by trying to make them do as they ought to. They are poor, ignorant, lazy creatures, who have very little motive or inducement to do well. We must make great allowance for them. We must do this for our own peace and comfort. If we make a fuss and get into a passion every time they do wrong, our lives will be continued scenes of unhappiness.

I hope you have taken the children with you to your mother's. Some accident might happen to them at home, in your absence.

I suppose you and Susan are pretty well prepared for the wedding by this time. I think your mother ought to convert her dining room into a chamber and eat in the basement story. Those rooms will suit for the purpose better than for chambers.

I wish you would tell Jim to sow the wheat, rye and barley in the best spots at the foot of the hill in the field, and leave the top and side of the hill for oats. Jim will understand.

I have caught a bad cold riding through the wind on Sunday. It distresses me a great deal. There was great danger from the falling of trees and limbs, on Sunday. The wind was very high. Several trees fell across the road.

I have been employed in a number of profitable and important cases, which will come on next court.

I must now conclude and think of my argument in the morning.   Yours truly,   B. F. PERRY.

PICKENS C. H., Thursday Morning.

MY DEAR LIZ: I have only time to write you a line by Colonel Townes. There is a great deal of business in court and I shall not be able to leave here until court adjourns, which will not be before Saturday. I may not get home before Sunday evening. As soon, however, as court adjourns I shall start; but I am afraid we will not get through the business even on Saturday evening.

General Whitner is unwell, and in consequence of it the case of infanticide will not be tried this court. I have a headache and an ugly boil on my nose, which gives me some pain and a great deal of uneasiness.

We were all considerably alarmed on Tuesday with an apprehension of the smallpox. Colonel Harleston came to court and whilst sitting in the Court House was taken ill and had many symptoms of that disease. He retired to his room and was unwell all night; but yesterday he was pretty well and went home, to our relief very much. He had a violent cold and some fever—nothing more.

I hope you and the children are well and getting on well. I need not tell you how anxious I am to see you all again. I have not seen any of my relatives, but have heard they are all well.

I hope you are by this time satisfied with your minister.

I have a great deal of business and have done well this court. I find my business here is increasing very considerably. We are now in the midst of an important slander case and have another one in immediate succession.

In great haste I am truly yours. Kiss the children for me.

B. F. PERRY.

PICKENS, Thursday Morning.

MY DEAR LIZ: I have only a moment to write you before Mr. Speer starts.

We are still in the case of Kirksey, and there is no hope of my being at home before Sunday, and this I regret very much. I am exceedingly anxious to see you and the children again, and I have been uneasy and unwell ever since I left home. It would be a great comfort to me to be permitted to stay at home altogether.

Kiss the children for me, and tell them how much I wish to see them.   Yours truly,   B. F. PERRY.

PICKENS C. H., Thursday Morning.

MY DEAR LIZ: I have barely time to say to you that I shall be here until Sunday morning. I hope you and the children are all well. I shall expect to see Will up when I return.

I have a great deal of business here, and so far have been successful. Mr. Speer is starting.

Yours truly,   B. F. PERRY.

PICKENS C. H., Monday Night.

MY DEAR LIZ: I am indebted to you for two very interesting letters, and I should have answered the first one by Sunday's mail, but I had not time. The stage arrived at Anderson after 12 o'clock. I then ate dinner and got started to my mother's by *one*. Drove thirty-two miles and reached there after seven, over a rough road, as you well remember.

I found my mother quite emaciated and helpless, confined to her bed. For a few minutes she did sit up, Sunday morning. In bed she was unable to turn over and had a dreadful cough. But her spirits and feelings are remarkable. She seemed contented and complained of nothing, talked cheerfully and manifested great interest in you and the children; said Josiah told her that Frank was the prettiest child we had, but she could not believe anyone so pretty as Will. Josiah was there, and poor fellow, his misfortunes still go on. He had a negro girl burnt to death last week. She was about 12 years old; caught fire in the field.

I did not see any of Foster's family. He had gone to Augusta to sell his cotton. I called at his house on my way to Pickens, but they were all off to church and I did not get out of my buggy. The rain was falling rapidly.

I drove in the rain Sunday three hours without dinner, and got a little wet. That night I felt unwell and this morning no better till dinner; since then I have been quite restored. Whilst driving my race mare in the night, over that bad road to my mother's, I felt a little unsafe; but there was no house to stop at.

At Anderson we were three days trying the case of Mattison and Clements. We were in court until midnight, Friday. I have the consolation of knowing that I made a good speech, although I lost the case. We have taken an appeal and may get a new trial. The testimony was in our favor, but the jury were all prejudiced against Mattison. The proof showed insanity: he saw God Almighty and was told he must marry Polly or die; the clocks talked to him, the witches whipped him; he saw visions and spirits, etc.

I have done pretty well in receiving money; have collected

$250 and have a prospect of getting $300 or $400 more. I have got some more business.

I did not see or hear from Mr. and Mrs. Sharpe. I read so much of your letter as was about the children to my mother, and told her Will learnt fast. She inquired whether he made good progress in his studies.

I do not know when I shall be at home—the last of the week sometime, and would be willing to be in the midst of your house-cleaning and confusion.

I hope everything goes on well at the farm. Be careful about the children and the fire—there is great danger. Be careful about yourself. There is danger in over-fatiguing yourself, in arranging the house, etc.

I must now conclude, as it is late and I have my room full of persons on business. Kiss the children.

Your loving husband,   B. F. PERRY.

SPARTANBURG C. H., Tuesday Morning.

MY DEAR LIZ: I have time to write you a line by Mr. Beattie. Judge O'Neal is quite sick with chills and fever. He has not yet been able to hold court, and we are all waiting on him. He came into court this morning and adjourned till to-morrow. If he is better we may go on with the business. If he is not we shall adjourn the court entirely. I may be at home to-morrow, and perhaps not till Sunday.

I hope you and the children are all well and doing well. Kiss them all for me. In great haste,

Yours truly and affectionately,   B. F. PERRY.

SPARTANBURG C. H., Wednesday Morning.

MY DEAR LIZ: Having an opportunity of writing you a few lines by Mr. Earle, I avail myself of it, although I have nothing to tell you except I am very anxious to return home. I do not know when I shall do so, perhaps not till Friday or

Saturday. I have a case or Mr. Kilgore which will detain me the greater part of the week.

I hope you and the children are all well and doing well. I suppose you are having the room, etc., whitewashed, purchasing summer clothes for the servants, etc.

The weather has been dreadfully hot. I had to take off my flannel and boots. I have also purchased of Heast a fine pair of boots and shoes, and I had to buy three pairs of cotton socks in order to be comfortable.

Colonel Nesbit offers to sell old George, and offers him for $300. He says George is very anxious to return to Greenville and expresses great affection for his wife in Greenville. I do not know but it would be a good plan to buy George for a gardener and cook.

In haste. Kiss the children for me.

Yours, etc.,   B. F. Perry.

Spartanburg C. H., Thursday Morning.

My Dear Liz: I will write you a line by General Thompson, who goes to Greenville this morning, as I do not know when I shall be able to get off, perhaps not till Sunday morning. I have a case of Kilgore's, which is at the foot of the docket, and I must remain to dispose of it. I shall be at home Sunday, if I have to return next week to the Court of Equity. They are progressing very slowly with the business of the Court.

General Thompson and myself went Tuesday evening to the Limestone Springs and returned the next morning. I saw there Colonel Elmore and family, Chancellor Job Johnston and his young wife—as young as his youngest children. She is quite pretty. Chancellor David Johnston and his daughter were also there and a Miss Hart, from Columbia. This was all the company.

The crops between Greenville and the Limestone Springs are terrible to think of. A famine seems inevitable. They are making nothing, and hundreds will suffer, if not perish.

Yesterday evening we all dined with Major Henry. He gave quite a handsome dinner.

I should like to have you and the children around me, this morning. It is worth while being absent from you to enjoy the pleasure of meeting again; and whilst we are always together we never know how deep our feelings are. It is absence which makes us reflect and feel, or rather develops our feelings. The pleasure of returning home is to me always sincere and heartfelt. But more of this when we meet. I am now writing in the barroom—not a very sentimental place or one in which we have quiet enough to indulge in reflection.

Tell Will his Spartanburg friends inquire about him and wish I had him with me. Kiss Anna and Frank for me, and believe me,   Your affectionate husband,

B. F. PERRY.

P. S.: I have heard nothing from poor Josiah, and I am afraid to hear. I love him sincerely and he is worthy of a brother's love.

SPARTANBURG, Thursday Evening.

MY DEAR LIZ: I am afraid 1 shall be delayed here till Sunday, and may not get home till after Laurens court; but I will try and return by home.

Since I came here, I have been employed in several important cases. I assisted Mr. Young in a murder case and we acquitted the defendant. I have been employed in a very important case of Bobo and Maybin, of Columbia, and have just gained it. I am now waiting for the case of Mr. N. Breedlove, against Cannon, about a negro.

Mr. Kilgore has paid me $50, and I have received $18 in another case.

Delia is very weak, but says she feels better. I have not seen her but once since I came here.

In great haste, as I am afraid the mail will close.

I hope you and the children are all well and the servants are doing well.

Let Reuben and Mary go on ploughing in the oats.
Yours truly and affectionately, B. F. PERRY.

ANDERSON C. H., Wednesday.

MY DEAR LIZ: I have only time to write you that I do not know when I shall be able to return home. I have disposed of three of my cases and have one yet to try. It is an action of slander, and I cannot leave until it is disposed of. The business of the court will not be disposed of in the week.

I must get off to be at home Saturday evening, as I shall have to go directly to Pickens. I am very anxious to return home to see you and the children and to give instructions about my farm. I wish I had nothing to do but stay at home and attend to my farm.

I hope to hear from you Friday morning, and I trust you are all doing well—Will going to school, Anna and Frank playing quietly at home, the servants attending to their business, etc. Kiss the children for me.

Yours truly, etc., B. F. PERRY.

LAURENS C. H., Friday Morning.

MY DEAR LIZ: I received your letter yesterday morning, just as I was going into court. Colonel McNeely told me that he had mailed a letter for me at his office, and the driver told him one of my children was sick. You may imagine how distressed I was, and how much relieved when I opened the letter.

We are still in Dr. Anderson's case, I have to speak this morning. General Thompson spoke yesterday evening and leaves this morning. Sullivan and Young both follow me. The case will take pretty much the whole week. I am fearful of the result.

Captain Cunningham is about starting for Philadelphia for his family, who are still there. I saw his overseer yesterday.

I am glad you are spending your time pleasantly with your

mother and Susan. I hope the children are behaving well and learning fast.

I shall not be at home before Sunday evening, and must conclude my letter in order to think over my speech this morning.   Yours truly and sincerely,   B. F. PERRY.

LAURENS C. H., Friday Morning.

MY DEAR LIZ: I have barely time to write you a line. Yesterday we were engaged until half-past one o'clock in the night, trying a slander case of mine, and after all I lost it. General Thompson and myself were on one side and Colonel Irby and Mr. Young on the other. We have a similar case to try to-day. I shall not be at home before Sunday. The weather is bad and the roads terrible.

I feel very much the loss of sleep, this morning, and don't like losing my case; but I have the consolation of knowing that I discharged my duty, and for the consequences I am not responsible.

I shall be delighted to be at home again, free from the excitement of a court and with my dear Liz and children.
            Yours truly, etc.,   B. F. PERRY.

LAURENS C. H., Tuesday Night.

MY DEAR WIFE: I received several statements to-day which satisfy me I have been elected by a handsome majority. I hope your fears are now put to rest.

I shall be at home Friday morning, and I propose to give our wine party Saturday night. Can you make the necessary preparations? Send and get two or three large hams, and some large turkeys and some fowls and have some bread baked in proportion. You may also have pound cakes prepared, etc. The supper may be set in the piazza, the wine in the dining room. You will have to borrow wine glasses, tumblers and bottles. If you can make all these arrangements, do so.

I wish every voter in the village invited. This can be done, perhaps, after my return. The invitations may be extended

informally through friends. Saturday will be the day of the
Agricultural Fair and I can invite persons from the country.
You must prepare to entertain at least one hundred persons.

If you see proper you can request Colonel Hoke, Major
Jones, Mr. Lester, Mr. Wells and any others to invite the vil-
lagers as they may see them or send them word. Invite every
voter in the village and others from the country—Sam Earle,
Elias Earle, Waddle, Poinsett, Dr. Butler, etc., Brooks, Dr.
Williams, etc.

We can make quite a display of cake and wine on the tables
in the dining-room and have the cold meat and bread and
coffee out in the piazza.

But, my dear wife, if you think it will give you too much
trouble, I will have the wine alone and nothing else. I think
the party had better be on Saturday evening.

I am truly sorry that Colonel Townes is not elected. In this
district Simpson will beat 500 votes. Colonel Fair is elected.

We have very little business in court.

Yours truly, good-night, and kiss the children.

B. F. PERRY.

———

LAURENS C. H., Thursday Night, Oct. 17, 1844.

MY DEAR LIZ: I am much disappointed in not getting off
this evening for home. Indeed I am afraid I shall not be able
to leave here before Saturday morning, if then; but I must
be at home Saturday night. There is an important case
which detains me. I hope to try it to-morrow. It is one in
which I have been employed to assist Mr. Young.

How comes on our wine party? If you have not commenced
it, I shall be glad. If you have made preparations for it, you
must go on. Have all the people invited. Get Lester, Hoke,
Jones, Townes, Wells and others to extend the invitations.
Let all the country people be invited who are in the village on
Saturday, at the agricultural meeting. I will give another
party Tuesday night of court week.

You must get three of four dozen bottles and fill them with
wine—*Sherry, Madeira and Sicily Madeira.* You are a great
manager and can do all these things without me; but still I

would like to be at home to help you.

I received a letter from Hoke and Lester giving me a full return of the elections. My majority was very gratifying, but exactly as I had calculated. You must now admit I have a good judgment in elections. I made a calculation of the votes Sullivan and myself would get at *each* box, and I am correct within a *very* few votes. I hope you will never *worry* me again on that subject.

I am very anxious to get home and meet you and the children. It appears a long time since I left home, and an important event has happened.

I received a letter for you from Miss Pamela Cunningham, and a note to me with a box containing a cap. I will send you the letter by mail.

Good-night, my *dear* Liz. Kiss the children.

Yours, etc.,   B. F. PERRY.

COLUMBIA, S. C., Sunday Morning.

MY DEAR LIZ: I received your letter yesterday morning informing me of your invitation to the Cunningham's to meet me and spend Christmas with the family, and as you seem so anxious about going, I have no objections; but I should enjoy myself more to meet you and the children at home.

I have no doubt you would find a change and a journey pleasant and agreeable. You may therefore go down there as soon as you please and stay till I arrive; but I cannot stay more than one or two days. We will take Christmas dinner with them and start home the next day or the day after. This is the condition on which we go there.

Before you go down you must make Jim haul wood, and see that there is plenty of shucks, fodder and corn for the cattle. He will know how to procure it of Uncle Foster. Do not start in bad weather. If you go to Goldsmith's the first day, you had better start about one o'clock. The next day you must make an early start, for it is a long day's drive. Do not let Jim drive too fast.

If the weather is suitable, I wish the hogs killed before you go. They are eating too much corn. Have them killed and the meat taken care of. I have no objection to your lending Mr. Yancey my horse and buggy.

If you go to Mr. Cunningham's, you must send the carriage to Laurens Court House for me. I shall probably be at Laurens Court House on Sunday, the 22d of December. I will then stay at Captain Cunningham's Monday, Tuesday and Wednesday. Christmas falls on Wednesday and we will start home Thursday morning—longer I cannot stay. You had better start down a week or ten days before, or as soon as you please. I hope to hear from you again to-night and if so, I will write you another letter should anything occur.

I have just read the account of the torchlight possession in the Mountaineer. It is quite magnificent.

I dined with Dr. Gibbes the other day and was much pleased with his entertainment. I have spoken of his collection of minerals, paintings and curiosities in a letter to the Mountaineer.

In the Temperance Advocate you will see a very handsome compliment paid my address. I have bought some few books and among them "The Gift for 1845," containing Simms' story about Greenville.

I am glad to hear you are getting on well with the servants and children. But it is late in the night and I must close this letter. Kiss the children for me and believe me,

Your affectionate husband, B. F. PERRY.

Monday Morning.

My DEAR WIFE: I have broken open my letter this morning to say to you, "do just as you please" about going to Mr. Cunningham's. You can go as soon as you please and send Jim back to kill the hogs and salt up the meat. Let him ride one of the horses back and leave the carriage and other horse at Mr. Cunningham's; and when he returns for you he can drive my buggy and mare and lead the other horse, so that I may have an opportunity of getting back, for we all could not return in the carriage. This, after all, may be the best arrangement, and will suit you best, but select good weather for going down, and write me before you go and after

you get down, for I shall be anxious to hear how you got down.
                    Yours truly,   B. F. PERRY.

                                COLUMBIA, S. C., Sunday Night.
  MY DEAR LIZ: I will write you a few lines to-night, as I shall
not have an opportunity of doing so to-morrow, before the
mail closes. I sat down to write you a letter two hours since,
but persons have been calling at my room ever since, and I
now will have time only to write you a very hurried epistle.
  You have no doubt heard of the death of Mr. Wm. E. Hayne.
I was told of his paralysis by Colonel Bee, who came down
with us in the stage from Greenville. Mr. Henry L. Pinckney
informed me to-night that he was dead. This is a sad calam-
ity to his family and to your mother. It will now become
necessary for some one else to take charge of your mother's
bonds., etc. You have no doubt heard all the particulars.
  Mr. Pinckney informs me your cousin Francis Hayne was
married to Mr. Sharpe, but he said nothing further about the
match.
  We had a very pleasant ride down here in the stage. Ware,
Walker, Duncan, Col. Bee, Messrs. Young, Moore and Lester.
We ate up all of your cakes, etc., and your praises were highly
sounded as a good wife, in providing for us, etc. The stage
broke down with us about ten miles from Columbia, but we
mended it with poles and came on. In jumping out of the stage
I hurt Colonel Barnard Bee in the breast. He was in great
pain for awhile, but he is better. The Colonel apologized for
not calling to see us, etc. I found him quite a pleasant gentleman. He talked a great deal and about a great variety of
things, and amongst other things his relationship to you, etc.
  I have got a fine room at Maybin's, and Ware, Duncan and
Walker have another one all together. The house is greatly
improved and I am to keep the room as long as I wish it.
  It is thought that Aiken will be Governor.
  I have met a great many of my old friends, and they all
seem glad that I am in the Senate. Mr. Pope and Colonel
Fair have said that the *gentlemen* generally will consider me
as in some measure *their* representative, no matter in what
district they reside.

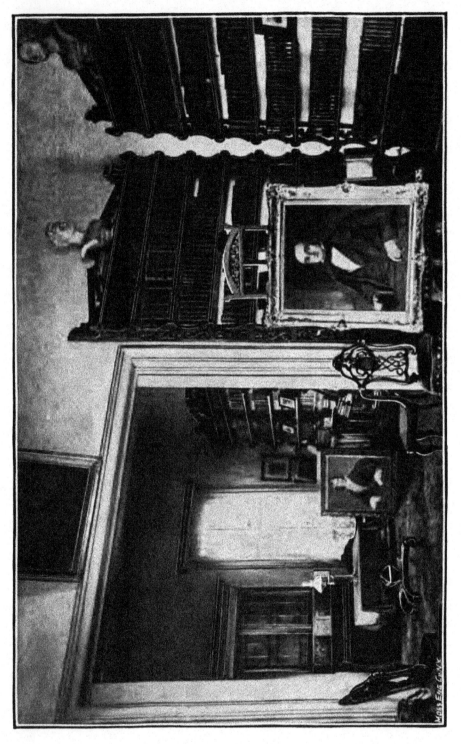

LIBRARY AT SANS-SOUCI

I hope to hear from you Wednesday night, and hear you are all well. I hope the children are well and that you have had no more scares. You are too easily frightened. Kiss the children for me. What about the torchlight procession?

Mr. Samuel Earle has just been in my room. His election I think pretty certain.

I must now bid you good-night. God bless you, my *dear* wife. Your loving husband, B. F. Perry.

Columbia, S. C., Tuesday Morning.

My Dear Liz: I must write you whenever I can, and therefore I will have to write the day before the stage leaves. I have a few moments of leisure this morning, before breakfast, and will avail myself of the opportunity of writing to my wife and children.

Yesterday morning I saw Colonel Martin, who said that Mr. Hayne's friends requested him to ask me to write and inform you of the particulars of his death. I told him I had already done so. I understand Mr. Hayne was in perfect health when the paralysis came on. He attempted to raise up a window and his right side became paralized and he fell to the floor. I hope, however, your mother has received letters from some of the family.

I made my *debut* in the Senate yesterday in a short speech on the contested election between Hibben and Rhett, which was well received. Have you seen the puff of me in the Charleston Courier? It was written by Gilmore Simms. Judge Frost told me yesterday he was really glad to see me in the Senate, and that my election gave great gratification to my friends in the lower country, and that they were *many*. Almost every one I have met has said to me that they were pleased to see me back in the Legislature. Colonel Pickens spoke to me as I went up to qualify, and said he was glad to meet me; that we had both got to be *old men* at the same time—alluding to our coming into the Senate together.

Judge Evans inquired very kindly after you, and so did Judges Butler and O'Neal. I gave the letter to Mr. Seabrook and also to Mr. Roper, both of whom inquired very kindly after you all, and Anne in particular. I had a long talk last night with Henry L. Pinckney, who also inquired after you all. He is very much like Frances Hayne. I could but think of Frances all the time I was talking to him; his nose, lips, expression of the eyes, etc. I found Pinckney a very pleasant man. His views and feelings, as expressed on every subject, were correct and honorable. He agreed with me very well in politics, and I was disposed to like him.

I have taken a seat in the Senate with Mr. Young. He left his seat and came over to where we both could sit together. I like Mr. Young very much. He is a noble fellow and *pure* hearted man. I *love purity* and *sincerity*, and will make *those only my friends* who *possess those qualities.*

The breakfast bell is now ringing, and I must close this very, very hasty scroll. I have bought the finest trunk you ever saw—a large traveling trunk ($22.) It will last us our lives and be a trunk for our children. I have also had to buy a cravat, pair of gloves, and shall have to purchase handkerchiefs.

You have no idea how much I wish to see you and the children and how glad I shall be to receive a letter from you. God bless you. B. F. P.

COLUMBIA, S. C., Wednesday Night.

MY DEAR LIZ: I have just received your letter written Sunday night. Major Butler goes up to Greenville in the morning, and has promised to carry this letter for me. I have therefore deferred writing to you till I could answer your letter by to-night's mail.

I am glad to hear you and the children are all well and the servants and animals are also well, and that you are all getting on well. You have before this time received my permission to go to Mr. Cunningham's, so you are well pleased on that subject; but really, I think you are going to make them a visitation with your children, servants and horses. You had better send Jim with one of the horses back, and when he returns for you he can drive down my horse and buggy and lead the horse behind the buggy.

I will send Susan's watch by Butler. he did not let me know

he was going until this evening, and I have had no opportunity of sending anything. The box I brought down I sent to Charleston by Elford, who promised to convey it to Mrs. Hayne. Elford told me that he and Sharpe are second cousins.

I saw Colonel Keith this evening, and he inquired very kindly after "Cousin Susan and her daughters." Mrs. Keith is with him. They are on a visit to her neice. Chancelor Harper in-inquired very kindly after Anne the other day.

I cannot give you any more particulars than I have, as to the death of Mr. Hayne. Colonel Taylor has gone down. I suppose his family were all present. His death is indeed a loss to his family and also to your mother. It would be proper for your mother to see about her bonds, etc., in his hands. She had better write to some one about it. If it is necessary, I will go to Charleston for her. She must write to me.

To-morrow I have to make my speech in the Senate on giving the election of electors to the people. I have already spoken several times, and I think I did pretty well. I feel some anxiety about my speech to-morrow. There is very little to do in the Senate—not one-half that is done in the House, nor is there one-half of the speaking.

A resolution was introduced to-day for the Legislature to adjourn until Monday, the 16th. This will interfere with our spending Christmas at Mr. Cunningham's. But I do not think the resolution will be agreed to. I have no idea that they will adjourn before Friday, the 20th.

I will send you "The Gift of 1845," by Butler, containing Simms' Greenville story. Moore and Lester will return to Greenville next Sunday night, and I will send my old trunk up by them, with some books in it, etc. They are to be examined to-morrow.

You need not talk to me about home! There is no place in the world so sweet as home, with your wife and children, and how I should like to be there to-night. God bless you. Kiss the children. I have a sore throat and cold.

Yours, etc.,   B. F. Perry.

COLUMBIA, S. C., Friday Morning.

MY DEAR LIZ: As I suppose you would like to hear from me, although I have nothing to write, I will not omit sending a letter by the mail, which closes this evening.

I have written to Wells pretty much all that we have done in the Senate, which you will see in the Mountaineer. But we do comparatively nothing in the Senate to what is done in the other House. Yesterday we had a short discussion on Colonel Pickens' resolutions. He came to me and asked me if I concurred with him, and on being told that I did, he requested me to reply to Colonel Moses, which I did in a short speech. After the Senate adjourned he requested me to ride with him in his carriage, and seemed very cordial and kind. He and the Rhett party have split and have no kind feelings for each other.

I received your letter by Wednesday's mail, and was much gratified to learn you were all well. How much I wished to be present and see you all arranged in the dining room whilst you were writing. Your description called everything to my mind very forcibly. There is no place like home, after all, especially when one has a wife and children at that home that they love so *ardently* as I do mine.

By the by, how do you come on with the servants? I hope they all behave themselves and give you no trouble. The children you can manage. How are the horses, cows and hogs? I hope Jim will take care of everything.

I saw Burt on his way to Washington. He seemed very glad to meet me. His hair and whiskers are turning gray most rapidly.

I think Mr. Aiken will be elected Governor, and I shall vote for him. I gave the letters to Messrs. Seabrook and Roper. Mr. Roper gave me one for your mother.

Mr. Sam Earle is not so good at electioneering as some of his competitors, and if he does not mind he will be hard pushed. The election between Elford and Butler is very uncertain. They are beginning to be a little excited with each other. Ware and Duncan are very much pleased with their situation, and I suppose Walker too. I never saw so many candidates before in my life. There are at least fifty to carry

the votes to Washington. Barclay's father came and spoke
to me and inquired after his son. He looks something like
his son and has the Scotch accent.

I have gained an important case—old Mr. McElroy's case
in Equity. You remember he once took *you* for *my daughter*.
I have succeeded entirely for the old man and am *proud* of it.
Mr. Sullivan was on the other side.

You see I have made up a letter in some sort of a way; so
God bless you and the children.

Your affectionate husband,   B. F. PERRY.

COLUMBIA, S. C., Friday Night.

MY DEAR WIFE: I have just received your letter and have
not much to write in reply.

All day I have been engaged in the Court of Appeals. All of
my cases have been disposed of except one, which I attend to
for Mr. Dean. The result of them I know not.

Yesterday was a day of great excitement in both Houses.
The members seemed to be crazy on the subject of the Massachusetts Mission. The House of Representatives passed a resolution expelling Mr. Hoar, with but one dissenting vote (Colonel Memminger.) In the Senate, *your husband* was the only
man who opposed them. I stood alone against the *whole*
Senate, and I made a most exciting speech. There were a
great many members who *thought* with me, but had not the
boldness to *act* with me. This vote has given Colonel Memminger and myself quite a distinction—*a minority of one.*

Mr. and Mrs. Roberts and Mr. and Mrs. Mauldin are here,
and will leave in the morning. I will send this letter by them.
I suppose you will be gone to Mr. Cunningham's before I write
to you again. I hope you will take good care of yourself and
the children and make Jim take care of the horses. When he
carries you down he can return and wait till the day before
Christmas, then go back to Cunningham's and drive down
my horse and buggy.

If I can, I will get Moore to take my old trunk up to Greenville with him. But there is such a crowd going up that I am
afraid he cannot do so.

Frank Burt has beaten Sam Earle for Treasurer. Colonel Anderson has been elected Superintendent of Public Works. The Governor's election comes on to-morrow. Aiken's chance is the best.

You must write me as soon as you arrive at Mr. Cunningham's. I shall feel very anxious to hear from you.

I have just had a visit from old George. He is cooking at Clark's Hotel. John's son Thomas also paid me a visit yesterday and inquired after his father. Thomas appears to be a very well disposed boy and looks pretty well, you can tell John.

I have written you so often that I have not much to write about, but will have the more to tell you when we meet, which will be the Sunday before Christmas, at the farthest.

God bless you and the dear children. Kiss them all for me. How I should like to see them!

Yours truly, my dear wife,   B. F. PERRY.

COLUMBIA, S. C., Dec. 8th, 1844.

MY DEAR WIFE: I received your letter this evening and it gave me pleasure.

I think a little recreation would be of service to you and the children. I have no doubt you would enjoy a short visit to Mr. Cunningham's, and I desire you to go, provided the weather is good. But do not think of traveling in bad weather. Select your time, and start when the weather is settled. You can go Thursday or Friday if you see proper. Jim can return home and bring down my buggy. I shall be at Laurens Court House Sunday 22d, in the morning. It may be that the Legislature will adjourn before that day, or rather so that I may be there sooner, but this is uncertain. We will fix on that day. You can make Jim return by that time. I do not wish to stay longer than three days at Cunningham's, nor will I. If you go down there it will be out of the question for you to leave Cunningham's before I come for you. They will not let you.

The election for Governor is over. Aiken is elected after five ballotings. He gave a treat the evening after his election, but it was not equal to yours.

I have been writing to a great many of my constituents since I have been here—Major Berry, Colonel Brockman, Colonel Johnston, Major Goodlett, Blasingame, Whitten, Colonel Barton, Dr. Crook, Dr. Irvine, Oliver Barrett and others. I have sent documents to a great many. So you see I am following your advice.

I met Governor Richardson the other day, who said he did not know I was old enough to be in the Senate. Every one congratulates me on my appearance, so I think I must be getting younger.

Mr. Wells has not received one of my letters, or, if he did, he has not published it; the letter contains the second and third days proceedings of the Legislature, in which I mention Colonel Maybin's hotel, etc.

I was disappointed in sending my trunk by last stage as it was full and Moore did not go up in the stage. I hope you have seen Mr. and Mrs. Mauldin and Mr. and Mrs. Roberts. I saw them whilst here.

I am glad to hear that Will learns better than he did. I have not yet purchased the presents.

Whenever I look at Colonel McWillie I am reminded of Frank. They look very much alike.

Colonel Ware, Duncan and Walker are all well. I have no further news to write you. God bless you and the children. Good-night.

Your husband,   B. F. Perry.

Columbia, S. C., Dec. 9th, 1844.

My Dear Wife: I have just seen Mr. Burt, who informs me that he will go up in the Greenville stage to-morrow morning. This gives me an opportunity of writing you again. put a letter in the postoffice for you this morning. Since that time the Legislature has determined to adjourn on Wednesday, the 18th; so I shall be at Laurens Court House Friday morning, the 20th. If you go down to Cunningham's you must make arrangements to send for me on that day to Laurens Court House.

I do not believe that we shall be able to take Christmas din-

ner with Mr. Cunningham. It will be too long for me to stay.
We can spend a day or two there after I arrive, and then
come on home. This will do just as well as to spend Christmas with them. You had better start down the day after
you receive this letter, if the weather be good; but if the
weather is bad, do not go at all.

I understand you have scarlet fever in the village. Mrs.
Walker writes to her dearly beloved that their son has had it
very badly. Be careful about the children catching it, and
take good care of them on the road.

I have been in court to-day and have gained Mrs. Field's
case, also another from Pickens, in which three men were con-
victed of hog stealing. My other cases not yet decided. This
case of Mrs. Field's will be worth $100 more to me by a new
trial. I now have to go down to the State House to attend
the Committee on Finance and Banks, of which I am Chairman, so I must close this letter.

In regard to your visit, do as you please; go when you
please, but do not travel in bad weather.

Your husband, with love and affection,

B. F. PERRY.

COLUMBIA, S. C., December, Friday, 1844.

MY DEAR LIZ: I hope you have arrived safely at Mr. Cunningham's, and I shall therefore address this letter to Water-
loo. I feel anxious to hear how you and the children made
out in your journey. But you are a great *manager* and I
have no doubt got on very well. You have beautiful weather.
By the by, you are this morning, about this time, 8 o'clock,
setting off from Goldsmith's.

I did not write you by the last mail, because I knew the letter could not reach Greenville before you had started, nor
had I time to write. I have been excessively engaged for several days past, and shall still be until the Legislature adjourns, and you may not perhaps hear from me again.

My bill giving the election of *electors* to the people has un-
dergone a long discussion and been rejected in the Senate by
a vote of twenty-five to seventeen. I opened the debate. Colonel Pickens replied in a very warm and excellent speech on

his side. Colonel Thompson spoke next, on my side. Colonel Dargan replied on the other side, in a long and most elaborate speech. This excited me to another effort. Colonel Preston came to me in the Senate Chamber, and gave me his views and went off and hunted up all the authorities for me. He brought young Mr. Blanding and introduced him to me, who also furnished me with some additional facts. The debate was adjourned till next day. In the meantime, Colonel Preston sent me more books. I went back fully prepared and made a speech of an hour and a half in length, which all friends and opponents admit did me great credit. A great many persons have appealed to me to have the speech published. I shall do so as soon as I have time to write it off. The Senate Chamber was almost empty when I took the floor. Before I concluded there was a dense crowd all around me, listening with profound attention. I felt that I was making a good speech, and my replies to Colonel Dargan and Colonel Pickens were very happy and appropriate.

I will now give you an account of two parties which I attended last night and the night before. The Governor, after his inauguration, gave a magnificent *democratic* party at Colonel Maybin's hotel. There were a thousand persons present. They drank eighteen hundred bottles of champagne, besides other wines and brandy! The supper was a handsome one and must have cost a great deal. The drawing-room was covered around the walls with flags, banners, transparencies, etc. There was a painting in one end of the room with the names of all the Governors of South Carolina, with Aiken at their head, showing through a transparency.

There were not many ladies. The Hamptons and Singletons were there, however, and some others. Before night I received a message from a lady that she desired to be introduced to me that evening at the Governor's party. So I brushed up and went into the ball-room about 10 o'clock, after returning from the State House. I was escorted through an almost impenetrable crowd to Mrs. Ellett, the wife of a professor in college, and a very literary lady who writes for all the magazines, reviews, etc. You have seen many of her articles in the Democratic Review. She is not only *literary*, but very *handsome*, about thirty—I believe ladies never get beyond that age. She took my arm and we commenced a promenade in the long piazza. The other ladies and gentlemen followed. We had quite a *literary* talk I found her very agreeable. She made me promise to collect some information connected with Colonel Cleveland's life and character.

Whilst promenading with Mrs. Ellett I met General Canty with a lady on his arm—about forty, with a pleasant, smiling face, bearing still the vestiges of former beauty. I thought I had seen her, but could not recall either name, time or place. In the course of the evening I asked General Canty who she was. He said to me, "She is an acquaintance of yours. Says she remembers you very well, and that perhaps you might remember her as *Mrs. Cripps.*" I took the General's arm and was immediately introduced to her. I saw her fifteen or sixteen years ago, at William Mauldin's wedding in Georgetown. She told me that she had frequently seen me since. She once heard me make a speech in the Legislature on the Duelling Bill; that she saw me at Greenville, etc. Poor woman! You know her sad fate: married, as her second husband, a drunkard, and separated.

Last night I received an invitation from Colonel and the Misses Hampton. Colonel Harleston and myself went together—four miles and a half. We started after 8 o'clock, got lost and arrived there just at 10 o'clock—quite a fashionable hour! When we came within a half mile of the house we saw immense torchlights on each side of the road and negroes standing to add fuel. The road was perfectly lighted. On the gate posts, a quarter of a mile from the house, there were large lamps burning. The lawn leading up to the house and all the circuitous walks in front of the house were lighted with lamps. I suppose at least one thousand. It looked like the starry firmament—brilliant indeed. Colonel Hampton's residence is a magnificent one and looks like an English nobleman's palace. I cannot undertake to describe it to you in a letter. The company had all assembled. We were asked into a wide entry, and on each hand there appeared to be rooms, as far as the eye could see. Filled with all the *elite* of Columbia, the Legislature and a large portion of the State.

There were wealth, and fashion, and beauty. Colonel Hampton met us and carried us through the smiling crowd to his daughters and gave us an introduction. They were dancing, waltzing and flirting, and talking all around. I knew most of the gentlemen present, but few of the ladies. I saw a lady dancing with Middleton who looked pretty, but somewhat faded, and I said to Mr. Bull, who was standing by my side, "What lady is that dancing with Middleton?" "That is Mrs. Bull," was his reply. I saw Miss Pride. She went to Europe the last season, with Colonel Davie. Your cousin Alston Hayne was there and quite a dancer.

The supper was the most bountiful affair I ever saw—magnificent yet *graceful*. The tables were arranged in circles all around the room; in the center a splendid column of evergreens, etc. But I will not describe. Leave this for a conversation. I left as the company were breaking up, at 1 o'clock, got home at two, and woke up this morning at six. Feel quite well. Have to be in the Court House at 10, to argue a case from Spartanburg, and in the Senate at 11.

Since I have been writing it has clouded over and we have appearance of rain. I feel for you and the dear little children and think of your lonely condition on the road. I hope however, it will not rain to-day. This day week I shall meet you, and I assure you that I shall quit this place with great pleasure. After my return home I shall have to go to Charleston, perhaps in January, to argue a case in the Court of Appeals—Mrs. Mayrant's case. The court has not time to dispose of it here. Colonel Hunt and the Attorney General are employed against me. We have made an arrangement to take it up whenever I go down. What say you to going with me? Now is your time. The only objection is the season of the year, but that is nothing if you go down in the stage. Think of it. We can carry *all* the children with us.

I must now go into court. You must give my respects to Mr. and Mrs. Cunningham and Miss Pamela. Tell her I have given her manuscript to Dr. Arnold. My friend Simms is about starting a magazine again. If he does, it will afford Miss Pamela and myself an opportunity of making use of the manuscript. Kiss all the children for me and believe me,

Your affectionate husband, B. F. Perry.

COLUMBIA, S. C., May 30, 1844.

MY DEAR LIZ: The mail closes to-morrow evening, and in the morning I shall be busy, so I must write you to-night. It is better to hear from me a day too soon than not at all. I hope to hear from you to-morrow evening. If I do not I shall be sadly disappointed.

I have made a considerable purchase of books, law and miscellaneous, and Mr. McCarter, the bookseller, is so much pleased with my custom that he has made *you* a handsome present. I do not know what it is, but it is a large book of pictures. He has wrapped it up and put it with my other books. I thought it would not be right to ask him what it was. It looks like it might be "Lady Blessington's Book of Beauties."

I have been trying to get a hat for Will, but they are rather small. I think you must have given me too large a measure. I see some beautiful Leghorn hats, about one inch smaller than your measure. Write me whether they will do. It seems to me that they will.

I saw Colonel Herndon's wife the other day; met her and him in the streets. She is good-looking, genteel and rather handsome, and possesses an intelligent face. Her appearance was simple and modest, and I was pleased with the glance I had of her. I must go and call on her before I leave.

I saw General Thompson this morning in court. He goes on Thursday next. I have seen nothing of Mrs. Thompson since I wrote you, nor have I seen Taylor or wife and family.

I do not know when I shall return. It is very doubtful whether any of my cases will be reached at all this court. I may stay till the last of next week, and all for nothing.

I have drawn the Bill in Equity for Mr. Watson against S. Mayrant; but Chancellor Harper is sick and they are not likely to have any court at Sumter. It is very doubtful whether Chancellor Harper will ever be able to take the Circuit again. He is now at the Glenn Springs and has not been able to come here. Judge O'Neal is also unwell, but is in court. Judge Evans looks very well and inquired particularly after you. Judge Frost looks well. I told him I thought his judicial honors agreed with him. Judge Butler looks a little rough.

We have now a fine rain falling, and it has been pleasant every day since I have been here. Mr. Young has gone to Charleston and says he may not be able to pay me.

I have bought me some law paper, also a very neat little shaving or dressing case, with all the appurtenances.

What presents shall I bring you and the children? A doll for Anna, hat for Will, a rattle for Frank and Mr. McCarter's book of pictures for you? Will that do? I want to see you and the children very much. How often I think of you in the midst of business!—and I have been very busy since I have been here. Mr. Dean has sent me some cases to attend to in the Court of Appeals, and says I shall be well paid if successful; Leitner has sent me some; I have some for Townes, and Young has left some of his with me; so I am a sort of general agent. Good-night.   Yours truly,   B. F. Perry.

I am on the committee to examine law students to-morrow.

LAURENS C. H., March 11th, 1845.

MY DEAR LIZ: It is now half after 10 o'clock in the night, and I have just finished my pleadings in three several cases of slander which are to be tried here this week.

I write you a line to inform you that I may not be at home till the latter part of the week. I have been employed to-day in the management of an important case and we are to argue it to-morrow. Young and myself on one side and Irby and Sullivan on the other. My fees will be $100. I have been employed in four other cases of great importance. Three of them will probably be tried this court and the fourth next court. I have also another case here in which I was employed last court, and a case of some importance. It will likewise be tried this week. You perceive I am doing well from home. My practice here is valuable to me.

I am very anxious to hear from you and the children, but suppose and hope you are all better. If the children become worse, you must write to me and I will return immediately.

Judge Wardlaw is presiding, and I find him pleasant and

agreeable. I have not seen or heard from Mr. Cunningham. As soon as I can possibly leave here I will, but that is very uncertain. I have nothing worth writing and it is so late I must conclude.   Yours truly and affectionately,

B. F. PERRY.

LAURENS C. H., Tuesday Night.

MY DEAR LIZ: I have sat down to thank you for your very acceptable letter this evening by Dr. Palmer. It contains a great deal of news and gave me great satisfaction. When from home I am always anxious to know how you and the children are doing, and nothing gives me more pleasure than such information.

I had the pleasure, as you requested in your letter, of being polite to Mrs. Palmer. I had her invited to sup with the Judge and lawyers. She sat next to me at the table, and we had considerable talk. The Doctor seemed quite sociable also. Mrs. Palmer told of you and your mother's cake, etc. The company is all gone from the Mansion House. I was in court and did not see the Middletons as they passed down in the stage.

Judge Frost came up in the stage, and lost between Newberry and this place his trunk with all of his clothes and $150 in cash. The trunk dropped off the stage. He sent back for it, but can hear nothing of it. Some one has picked it up and appropriated it, leaving the Judge without a clean shirt and nothing but a very shabby suit of clothes on his back. I lent him my razor and offered him a shirt, but he procured one from the store and has a shirt washed every day. He says he will make Captain Ward pay for his loss. The straps of the leather boot containing his trunk were not buckled. He is a very pleasant, agreeable gentleman, and a pretty good Judge.

I received a short letter from Miss Pamela this morning, with a package of books for her Greenville subscribers, and amongst them is Mrs. Poinsett. You say Mrs. P. is not a subscriber. I have a book for her anyhow. Pamela writes from Abbeville C. H., and is still very feeble. Sends her love to you and the children and wishes you to copy from my Curwen Journal all

the corrections she made with a pen into the copies sent her
Greenville subscribers. The indictment against Mr. Cunningham for whipping young Bowen is going on and will be tried
next court.

I received a letter to-day from Sam Earle on the subject of
the railroad, etc. The people do not seem to take much interest in the matter here. They are all absorbed in the corn
meetings, etc.

None of my cases have been tried yet, and I shall be here all
the week.

General Thompson told me as we came down that Butler
and Miss Jones were going to be married.

I have exchanged my gold chain for another one. It broke,
and I found all the links were wearing and worn out. I have
a very beautiful one in exchange, something like yours, and
I gave $4 to boot. I hope you have received and taken care
of my plows and straw cutter. As President of the Agricultural Society I shall have the honor of introducing the first
subsoil plow ever in Greenville district, and also the first plow
of another description. I bought them to use and show at
the agricultural meeting and Fair. I have received a present
of a valuable book on agricultural chemistry, by Johnston.

Tell the servants to gather the peas and clear as much as
possible before I get home. Thank Frank for his letter. General Thompson saw him beating the drum on Saturday and
says he is a "*born Democrat.*" Tell Anna and Frank howdy
and kiss them all. Miss Crawford's expression is in character, and the next time let her invitation be delayed still longer. The news from Colonel Hoke is good. I am "grateful"
to you for your letter. Good-night—near 10 o'clock.

Your affectionate husband,   B. F. Perry.

LAURENS C. H., Thursday Night.

MY DEAR LIZ: As I shall not be able to return home before
Sunday, I will write you a few lines. Nothing yet has been
done with my cases, and I am very tired of waiting. My
great apprehension is that after staying all the week I shall

not be able to reach them. I have three very important slander cases and the great Will case all ready for trial.

I saw Mr. and Mrs. Allston and Miss Gadsden last night. They spoke highly of you and your kindness to them, praised Will, etc. I see a good many persons passing down the country. The dancing master *Fugiss* went on this morning.

I have procured a box of seeds and wheat of an extraordinary character which was ordered from the North. I will now plant wheat this fall, which I did not intend doing, but which you wished me to do. The grass seeds I am lucky in getting. I have had a great deal of agricultural talk with Judge Frost. It is now after 11 o'clock.

It would give me great pleasure if I was at home with you and the children. My farm is now another inducement to be at home. My wife, my children, my office and my farm are all great attractions for me—the office the least of all and yet the most *profitable*.

I hope John is well, so I can put Charles to work when I return.

It is so late in the night I must conclude. In the morning, if I have time, I will write a note to Will and Anna and Frank.

Yours truly and affectionately. Good-night,

B. F. PERRY.

COLUMBIA, S. C., May 10th, 1845.

MY DEAR LIZ: I have just seen the Postmaster and requested him to let me mail a letter, although the hour has expired. I have therefore but a few minutes to write you in.

You did not write me by the last mail, but Colonel Butler and Rowland informed me that you were all well. They inform me of the very sudden death of Mrs. Chick.

From present appearances we shall not be able to reach the cases at all from the Western Circuit, and if so you may look for me at home Friday night. I will have to stay till Wednesday, as I am on the committee to examine students on that day. We shall then determine whether it is worth while for us to stay or not any longer. The Court of Errors will occupy two weeks and the remainder of the month will be consumed with the Southern and Middle Circuits. My business in the Court of Errors is through with.

I have purchased a pair of candlesticks for chamber use, price $4. My other purchases you are informed of and you did not desire anything in your last letter. By the by, your letter was one of great interest and gave me much pleasure. Your troubles now are War and your Box. I suppose Butler Thompson has returned before this time and relieved you of the latter trouble. In regard to the first, you need be under no dread.

I wrote Wells a long letter for The Mountaineer yesterday and went to church, which is the reason I did not write you —but I had nothing to write about.

I saw Dr. Davis last week, who said he wished me to ride out some evening and see him.

The lawyers from the country are now coming in. Colonel Fair came down this morning Butler and Rowland go to Charleston in the morning and will return the last of the week.

I would give a great deal to see you and the children. It would never do for me to be a member of Congress. I should find it impossible to stay in Washington the whole winter unless you and the children were with me.

We have had a fine rain, and I was truly glad to hear you had rain in Greenville. The rain is now falling and I must conclude my letter and send it to the postoffice, or it will not reach Greenville before I do myself.

Kiss the children for me. and tell them I will bring them all something.   Yours truly, etc.,
                                             B. F. PERRY.

COLUMBIA, S. C., May, Wednesday.

MY DEAR LIZ: I have only time to write you a few lines. and I hope to hear from you this evening. There are so many of you at home that I feel more interest in hearing from you than you can possibly feel in hearing from me. You or some of the children may be sick or something may have happened. This always makes me anxious to hear from you every mail, when absent from home.

I have been very much engaged since I have been here. Two of my cases in the Court of Errors have been argued and a third will be to-morrow. I shall then be at leisure until the appeals from the Western Circuit are taken up, which I fear will not be for two weeks. Mr. Young was sick and did not come down with me in the stage. I engaged Colonel Preston to take his place on our will case from Laurens. Colonel Preston had a similar case from Union and was therefore prepared. He made a fine argument and I think I did the same, and we hope to gain the case, but all things are uncertain in law.

The Charleston lawyers are here—Pettigru, Baily, Memminger, etc. I find Colonel Martin here also, and the Beaufort lawyers. Martin has a big will case, also, in the Court of Errors, in which he and Pettigru will get a fee of $2,000 or $3,000, if they succeed. That, however, is very doubtful.

I have bought you "Notes on Cuba" and "Housekeeping." The beads and soap not yet purchased, but shall be. I have also engaged me a suit of summer clothes, very genteel and from a very fashionable tailor; price $39—sack coat.

Tell Will that his friend Mr. Summer inquired very kindly about him and says the puppies shall be sent him next fall. He asked me why I did not bring Will with me.

Mr. Barclay called to see me last night and says he is coming to Greenville this summer and will expect to take your portrait.

Judge Richardson and Chancellor Harper are both absent and sick. Chancellor Dunkin told me he saw Colonel Arthur Hayne the other day, who told him he was going to Greenville shortly.

We had a very dusty time coming down. Sam Earle came with me and Judge O'Neall, from Newberry; also Colonel Irby. Mr. Elias Earle is still here. I did not get to see Colonel Coleman as he passed through Columbia.

I hope you and your household are getting on smoothly. Write me as often as you can and let me know what you are all doing, etc.

Kiss the children for me and tell Anna I will buy her a pretty frock and Will something. Tell Frank he must learn to talk before I return.   Yours truly and sincerely,

B. F. PERRY.

SANS-SOUCI.

COLUMBIA, S. C., Friday Morning, May, 1845.

MY DEAR LIZ: I hope to hear from you to-night. The last mail I had the same hope, but was disappointed. I will write you a few lines this morning, before I breakfast, so that you may not be disappointed on Sunday night.

But I have nothing to write except about my cases, and I am sure this must be rather a dull subject to you, however interesting it is to me whilst they are being tried. I know nothing as yet as to the result of any of them. Colonel Preston told me yesterday evening that the Judges were equally divided on Teague's Will, and that they would probably wait until they got a full court, and have it re-argued.

I went to Colonel Preston's office, yesterday evening, which is in an old and little building back of the Court House and in the second story. It was, altogether, a most comfortless looking room. I found the Colonel sitting alone, without coat, waistcoat or cravat. When I went in he put on an old Osnaburgh, hunting shirt. I could but think to myself, "Here is the great and eloquent South Carolina Senator who has made, and justly made, such a figure in the world!" We commenced talking about our cases and Mr. Pettigrew came in. They were preparing for an argument in a great case which comes on to-day about General Hamilton's property. Colonel Preston made, the day before yesterday, one of the finest and richest arguments I ever heard, in a case of Taylor vs. Taylor. The estate was worth $200,000. An old Englishman by the name of Taylor, some sixty or seventy years old, married a beautiful young lady about sixteen years old, by the name of Roberts, cousin of Miss Roberts, who was in Greenville summer before last. Taylor died leaving an infant child. He gave his wife the interest on $30,000 during her life, and the whole estate to his child. The widow was trying to break the will and is now engaged to be married. Her intended husband was a witness in the case and resides in Savannah. If the will is broken she will get $70,000 to dispose of as she pleases, instead of the interest on $30,000. Mr. Pettigru said it was "a contest between *youth and beauty* on the one side, and *age and jealousy* on the other." This is the case in which Colonel Martin is engaged.

I have disposed of all my cases in the Court of Errors and am now waiting for those in the Court of Appeals. I have been very much interested and edified by the arguments which have been made by Preston, Pettigru, DeTreville, Bailey and Colcock. It is a fine school for a lawyer, and I am not able to say when I shall be able to return.

I have made the following additional purchases: two strands of beads, one for you and one for Susan; three cakes of Marine soap and two cakes of Chinese soap—all floating soap; a pipe which is a real curiosity and will do for a chimney ornament, a pen knife, two bundles of perfumery to put in your clothes and a vial of perfumery. That is all.

Last night I went to hear the Orphean family sing, and was very much pleased. They are two men and two women, brothers and sisters—big, awkward Yankee people, and ugly withal—but they have wonderful voices. One of the family imitates the highest key of the piano, the flute, etc.

The weather is now cool and rather pleasant, but very dusty. If you wish me to get anything, write about it. I must get some present for Will. Tell him I should like to have him with me.

Breakfast is now ready and I must conclude.

Yours truly and sincerely,   B. F. PERRY.

PICKENS C. H., June 20, 1845.

MY DEAR LIZ: I have only time to write you a *line* by General Thompson and to thank you for your long letter. Willie is quite well and has behaved remarkably well. His grandmother was delighted to see him and so were all his relations, especially Foster's wife and family. He has been very much admired by all who have seen him. His only fault is that he will *stick* to me too closely.

I shall probably be at home to-morrow evening (Saturday.) One of my cases has been postponed and the other we are trying to-day.

You did not write me how much you subscribed to the church.

We have had a fine rain and I hope it extended to Greenville.   In great haste yours truly, etc.,

                                        B. F. Perry.

                    Laurens C. H., Monday Morning.

My Dear Liz: It is said that fortune seldom comes single-
handed. I left home yesterday with a heavy heart in consequence of Edward's sickness and my apprehension that it
might spread in the family. This morning I found my horse
badly foundered. After bleeding and doctoring him I stepped
to the branch, fell on a rock and *dislocated* and *broke* my left
arm at the wrist. I was all alone and with difficulty got back
to the hotel. Mr. Grymes came to my aid and assisted me to
the house. Dr. Henry was sent for and he bandaged each fin-
ger, the hand, wrist and arm. It gives me great pain. After
lying on the bed an hour I have got up to write you an account of the sad accident. I am too restless to remain in bed.
Perhaps I may be able to go into the Court House to-morrow.
It prevents me from attending to the solicitor business, but
Colonel Orr will do that. I have two cases on the issue
docket, and they may not be reached before Thursday or Friday. I do not know when my horse will be able to travel. I
may get some one to drive him up; but I will write you again.
Be quiet and easy. You know I am a philosopher and can
bear all that cannot be prevented by wisdom and prudence.
I am still able to write. as you perceive. It is fortunate that
it is my left arm instead of the right. I can still go on and
take testimony in Pickens next week. But I shall have to go
in the carriage and take Reuben.

I hope you and the children are all well and that Edward is
better. I pray to God that the fever may not spead in the
yard.

My fall was a very bad one. In crossing a little branch I
slipped on the rock and fell with the whole weight of my body
on the wrist. The doctor has just been to see me and thinks
I am doing well.   Yours truly and sincerely,

                                        B. F. Perry.

LAURENS C. H., Tuesday, 12 o'clock.

MY DEAR LIZ: I did not rest well last night. My arm gave me considerable pain. It still pains me, but I suppose this is unavoidable.

I got up this morning, however, and shaved myself, and with the assistance of Colonel Orr's boy, I dressed. I breakfasted at the table and had a servant to cut my food. After breakfast I walked to the horse lot to see my horse. He is pretty well over the founder and will do to drive to-morrow or the next day. I wish I could mend as fast. I went into court this morning at ten and have just returned from the Court House to my hotel. My cases cannot possibly be reached before Friday or Saturday, and I am very unwilling to remain that long. I saw Mr. Gower here just now. He proposed taking me up in his buggy. I could get McKay to drive my horse and buggy home.

I received your letter this morning, which gave me some comfort. But I am low-spirited and wish to be at home and especially out of a hotel, and where I can have my dear wife to contribute to my comfort by her attentions and society.

The election I hardly think of at all. I heard a cock and bull story of arrangements made to defeat Brockman, but it will only open the eyes of the people to the tricks and duplicity of the disunionists in Greenville and their friends and tools. I have heard nothing from the election.

In this district the contest will be very close between Irby and Calhoun.

I shall expect to hear from you to-morrow morning again, and every morning till I return home.

Kiss the children for me. I wish to see them and you very much, my darling wife.

Your affectionate husband,   B. F. PERRY.

LAURENS, C. H.

MY DEAR WILLIE: I was very much pleased to receive your letter. It shows that you think of and love your papa, although he is absent. The next time you write you must ask mamma to pencil the *words* and let you fill them up. This will make your letter more interesting.

You must learn fast and keep *head* whilst I am from home. Never let any of the little boys outspell you. I wish to see you a great man some day. So you must love your book and school. You must also try to be a good boy and mind what mamma says. Love Anna and Frank and be kind to the little boys at school. Never quarrel or fight.

If you do these things, papa and mamma will love you and everybody will be good to you, and you will grow up to be a great and good man.   Your papa,

                                               B. F. PERRY.

COLUMBIA, S. C., Sunday Night, Nov. 1845.

MY DEAR WIFE: I arrived here this evening, after a fatiguing passage in the stage, and have nothing of interest to write you. I am afraid if I have to postpone writing till to-morrow I shall not have time. As yet I have seen very few persons, but as I know you will be glad to receive a line from me saying I am well and have arrived safely, I will write you this evening.

We had a stage full—Elias Earle, Walker, Speer, Ware, Dr. Evans and Norriss, from Anderson. Colonel Ware joined us at McNeely's. He and Earle had provisions with them, and with mine we all made a sumptuous dinner yesterday and to-day. The tavern at Newberry C. H. has improved very much. By the by, Judge Frost has heard of his trunk. Some negroes of a man by the name of Holeman found it in the road and secreted it. They burnt the trunk and books, passed a portion of the money, dressed themselves in the Judge's clothes and gave his silk gown to a negro woman to wear. A portion only of the money has been recovered, and the gold watch and his new suit of clothes.

Mr. John Maxwell is a candidate for Superintendent of Public Works, which will interfere most seriously with Elias Earle's chances of success. Their friends are trying to persuade them not to both run. Mr. Maxwell is a rich man and does not need the office, but if he runs he will prove a very formidable competitor.

The feeling in favor of the railroad is strong from Greenville to this place, and the feeling in Charleston and other portions of the State is friendly and favorable. I think a charter will be obtained this session, but I am afraid the Legislature will not take stock in the road.

Duncan and McBee were just ahead of us and are at the house (Maybin's.) I suppose Luther and Susan will be married the day after you receive this letter. You are now no doubt busy in arranging for the wedding, and hardly have time to read my letter, so I will stop and write you a longer one next mail.

Tell Jim to kill the hogs as soon as the weather turns cold. We had rain Saturday night. Do not leave the children alone; I dreamed about it last night. Kiss them for me. Tell Willie to learn fast and I will buy him a pretty knife; Anna to be good and she shall have a present; and Frank must talk and be rewarded. God bless you, my dear wife.

Yours, etc.,   B. F. PERRY.

P. S.: Colonel Martin and Colonel Taylor inquired where you were. They had understood you were coming down with me. Mrs. Martin is not well, nor is Mrs. Taylor well.

I told Judge Butler that Susan was to be married. He said perhaps his advice had had some influence on her.

The weather is cold to-day (Monday) and clear.

I presented the Railroad Petitions and they were favorably received.   In haste, your affectionate husband,

B. F. PERRY.

COLUMBIA, Nov. 29th, 1845.

MY DEAR WIFE: I read your letter this evening and was extremely glad to hear you were all well. If your letters contain nothing else, they will nevertheless be read, and read with great pleasure. It would be gratifying to me if I could now take a peep at you and the children. Tell Will I have been looking at some knives for him, and he must write me a postscript to some of your letters. Colonel Ancrum has his little son with him, who is about Will's size and make, with hair exactly like Will's. With his back to me, I thought of him; but his face is not so intelligent and manly.

I carried your watch and pencil to the jeweler's this morning and he is to repair them. I saw some beautiful striped silk dresses to-day; would you like one? Your shoes I gave to Dr. Davis, and he is to exhibit them to-morrow night at the Agricultural meeting. Mr. Poinsett makes his speech then in the State House. I saw him yesterday in the Senate for a few minutes. There was a meeting last night of the State Agricultural Society. Judge O'Neall and Butler made speeches.

In the Legislature not much has yet been done. We elected Mr. Calhoun to-day in the place of Judge Huger. No other election takes place. Major Earle seems in good spirits. There are about twenty candidates for Superintendent. We have strong electioneering for Comptroller General. I have made up my mind to vote for Colonel Wigfall.

The speech I made last winter on the election of electors has been put in circulation to-day amongst the members by some one, and I have been complimented by some of the members for it. Some change will now have to be made on that subject. I do not know whether my speech has been reprinted or whether this addition has been put forth by the Chronicle.

The railroad is meeting with favor from all quarters.

I have been very busy for two days past in looking up law in McBee's case about the gold mine. Chancellor Johnson was hesitating on one point. I have now furnished him with law sufficient on that point and he will now decide in my favor.

To-morrow Susan is married, and before this reaches you another member will be added to your mother's family.

I am writing in a great hurry and Colonel Ware is waiting to take my letter to the postoffice.

Kiss the children and give my compliments to McBee and Susan.

Yours truly,   B. F. Perry.

COLUMBIA, S. C., Nov. 28th, 1845.

MY DEAR WIFE: I have just returned from dining at Dr. Gibbes', in company with Mr. Poinsett, the Governor, Judge Butler, Chancellor Dunkin, Chancellor Johnson, Messrs. Barnwell, Seabrook, Colonel Pickens, Col. Allston, Col. Preston, etc. The stage leaves in the morning and I must write tonight or you will not have the *pleasure* of hearing from me. The other evening I went with Major Henry to the postoffice and received your letter. He inquired how often we wrote to each other, and seemed astonished. He writes once in *two weeks*. I have just sent to the office for letters now, and hope to hear from you before I have finished writing. I spent a very pleasant and agreeable evening at Dr. Gibbes' and drank some most excellent wine.

Last night Mr. Poinsett made his agricultural speech before a crowded house of ladies and gentlemen. I met Mrs. Poinsett there, also Miss Blanding, by whom I was seated duduring the evening. She inquired after you with interest and seemed agreeably surprised when I told her Susan was to be married that evening. She called McBee her "old friend Luther." She seems quite a pleasant young lady. Our friend Gilmore Simms made a most flowery speech, complimenting the ladies and some domestic wine which a Miss Roberts presented to the Society. After he had concluded I observed to the meeting that my friend from Barnwell had omitted one thing. He should have offered his wine to the ladies after he finished making his speech, whereupon he came forward and did so, to the amusement of the meeting. Your shoes were greatly admired by Miss Blanding and other ladies who examined them in my presence. Dr. Gibbes reported on them, and this morning I carried them to have made up.

To-day I have been all day in the Court of Appeals arguing a case of Mr. Kilgore's. In the House of Representatives they had some speaking on Mr. Calhoun's course at the Memphis Convention. The members appeared like Calhoun's *slaves* and *refused* to assert their *opinions*.

The boy has just returned from the postoffice and brings no letters from you, which is a great disappointment; but I suppose you were so busied about the wedding that you hadn't time to write. I wish I could have been at it. Susan is, I hope, *happy*, as she should be and deserves to be. I think I heard some one say to-day that General Bonham was married.

Mr. Tom Cox was here to-day on his return from the North. Poor fellow, he looks rather sad. He goes up in the stage in the morning. He left Miss Skinner behind him.

I hope to see, next week, some one from Greenville, which will give me great pleasure. I should like to be there and see you and the children. I wish Will was here with me. Kiss Anna and Frank.

The weather is cold. I hope the meat is doing well. You must write me everything about the farm, the children, etc.

I must now bid you good-night. Give my congratulations to Susan and McBee.

Most devotedly, your husband, etc.,
B. F. Perry.

Columbia, S. C., December 1st, 1843.

My Dear Wife: I received your letter by Sunday's mail, informing me that Susan was married. Sunday night Mr. Elford came and brought me the wedding cake. I have distributed a portion of it amongst the Greenville delegation. The piece for Pinckney McBee has been handed to him. I informed him that we had become akin to each other since we left home. I saw Colonel Martin this morning in the Senate and informed him that I had a piece of cake for him and Taylor. He said he would send for it. Mrs. Martin is now at Taylor's. She arrived here Saturday evening. I promised to go and see her. Martin had his little son with him in church on Sunday, but I could not see him well.

General Thompson and Butler Thompson are at this house. They came Sunday evening. Butler talks very freely about his marriage and says he has it so arranged that I shall be at home when it takes place. General Bonham and his bride are in Columbia. I saw them to-day at the college commencement. They looked very happy. There was another bride sitting by Mrs. Bonham—Mrs. Randal, formerly Miss Lipscomb, now married to Mr. Pearson's cousin, of Chester or Fairfield.

Ben Yancey and his sister are in Columbia, but I have not seen them. I saw John Cunningham to-day. He says Pamela is much worse than she used to be, though better than she was in the summer. He spoke of her despondingly. Mr. and Mrs. Cunningham are well.

I have very little to write you about the Legislature. We have done very little yet, and there has been a motion to adjourn on the 12th, next Friday week. If you don't mind, I shall get home to your party. You wrote me to let you know the price of fruits. They are moderate in price. The oranges are not good. The pineapples are small and 25 cents by retail. The grapes are very delicious and packed up in little kegs. If you will direct me, I will make a purchase for you and send them up in the stage.

In spite of your advice to the contrary, I am becoming home-sick and would like very much to be with you and the children to-night. There is no place to me like home. I very often go from home most cheerfully, but I soon wish to return. The novelty and excitement of new scenes soon ceases to interest me; my wife and children never. It is true they sometimes interest me a little too much, but I never get tired of them, as I do of everything else in this world. I pity, from the bottom of my heart, him who has no wife and children. Here is Colonel Ashe, rich and surrounded by the world's wealth and luxury, but no wife or children. He seems to be without aim, object or interest.

I am glad you think yourself so happily married as to wish Susan the same degree of happiness. It is true we both have everything to make us happy. It has very seldom fallen to the lot of two persons, husband and wife, to have less alloy to their happiness. We enjoy uninterrupted health; we have been prosperous, living well, surrounded by and enjoying all the comforts of life, accumulating property, notwithstanding our extravagance, blessed with uncommon children—for I see none equal to them, and our love for and confidence in each other is all that husband or wife could wish or desire.

In regard to March, I hope you are mistaken. Jim has made

him work very hard at very hard work, splitting rails, and he is not accustomed to it and is young and slender. There is a great deal of *come out* in March when he fattens and fills up.

Write me whether any oats are sown, any fence made, how many rails made, how the hogs I bought of Watson do. This information you can get from Jim.

Colonel Martin has just come in and got his cake and brought me a bundle for Susan B. McCall—a small bundle like silk or calicoes,

I must conclude. I went to the Episcopal church last Sunday.

You will see the political news from me in the Mountaineer Friday morning.

Tell Willie I have seen some very pretty knives. Tell Anna she must tell me what to purchase for her. Tell Frank to say what he wants. I wish I had Will with me. Col. DeTreville has his little son with him. We walked back from the college together. He says he carries his son to let him see and hear things—to gain practical information of more value than lessons from books.

Write me what you want.

Yours truly and affectionately,   B. F. Perry.

Columbia, S. C., Dec. 3, 1845.

My Dear Wife: I have just finished writing questions for the students in Equity, who are to be examined to-morrow and I am one of the committee. It is now 8 o'clock and I have to put this letter in the postoffice to-night. The preparation of questions has given me a great deal of trouble, and I did not know of my appointment till this morning. There are four members of the Legislature and one member of Congress applying for admission in Equity.

I have just received your letter of Sunday night, and have the last letter also. It had been lost in the bar-room. Hereafter I shall take your advice and go to the office myself.

Your letter advising me not to purchase any fruit for you has come too late. This morning I started to you in Benson's wagon one hundred oranges, six cocoanuts, one dozen plantains, one dozen bananas, one keg of grapes—twenty-six pounds—delicious grapes; fifty cents worth of almonds, same of hazel nuts, same of Brazil nuts, one drum Smyrna figs, five pounds of candy, twelve pineapples, all costing $16.85. They are all in one box, except the grapes, which are in a keg. I have also sent a large box of books, law books, which I could not well do without. I have paid for them in part by an order on a client in Charleston. The balance I pay next winter. Jesse R. Young owed me $100 for a case at Laurens. The books cost me $315—and cheap at that price. I bought them of Messrs. McCarter & Allen. I know you will be surprised, but they are books I have long wanted and could not do well without. All that I have, and all that I ever expect to make, have been and will be the product of books. My books have been profitable and therefore I must enrich my Library. I will pay for the balance, $215, in some fees which I shall make pretty easily. Take good care of them and don't let the box get wet before you put it in the house.

You will receive the boxes and keg Tuesday next. Benson, Wade and Lark were all down here, hauling Gibbes' property down. Benson owes me and I have got him to take back the two boxes and keg. Elias Earle has also sent up some fruit. and Speer sent up a box full by the same wagon.

Tell Colonel Coleman that the Railroad Bill has been reported and read once in the Senate.

I introduced some resolutions to-day in the Senate on the subject of General Jackson, which I think beautifully drawn. They have been ordered to be printed and I will send you a copy.

I have not time to write you more at present. Kiss the children. Give my respects to your mother, Susan and Anne and McBee. Write me all about them. The weather is cold and bad.   Yours truly and affectionately,

B. F. PERRY.

COLUMBIA, S. C., Friday Night.

MY DEAR LIZ: I have just received your and Willie's letter and was very glad to hear from you, and especially pleased at Willie's first intelligible letter to me. Tell Willie I have not time to write, this mail, but will by the next. Indeed, all my letters to you have been written in great haste, because I always wait to receive your letter before writing, and I am so busy here that I hardly have time to do anything.

Last night the Governor gave a ball, but I had been busy in court all day, and had to meet a committee at night and did not go. I felt tired and went to bed about the time the others went to the ball (10 o'clock.) I had to be in court all day to-day, and knew that I should not feel well if I went to the Governor's.

The courts are now trying my cases and will be at it next Monday and Tuesday. To-day the law students were examined and all admitted (36), Pinckney McBee amongst them. The Equity students were all admitted yesterday, and they all complimented me very much for my courtesy and kindness to them in my examination of them. Butler Thompson is admitted in Equity, and Elford.

I had the pleasure of seeing Colonel Martin's two little boys this morning. They came with him to the State House. The oldest is a good-looking boy, so also is the second, but not equal to *our* Willie. In fact, I have never seen three children so sweet looking as ours. This I say independent of the influence of love and partiality. He has *five* children! What a charge for a poor man to have! I must go and see Mrs. Martin and Mrs. Taylor.

I saw your cousin Alston Hayne the other day and he promised to call and see me, but has not. I saw him in the Senate Chamber.

The election of Superintendent of Public Works comes on to-morrow at 1 o'clock. Mr. Elias Earle will soon know his fate. He seemed pleased at *your wish* for his success.

Pinckney McBee and B. Thompson start home to-morrow morning, but will go through Edgefield and will not reach Greenville before Thursday. General Thompson will start home the first of next week. Alston has gone to Charleston. Tom Butler and Rowland have not reached here yet.

My box of fruit and keg of grapes will reach you in time for your party, but the weather is so cold you will have an un_ pleasant time. Be careful about fire. Colonel F. Wardlaw got his house burnt up last week, by the rolling down of a chunk of wood on the floor. Have the fire attended to every night and be careful about the children falling into the fire.

How I should like to hear Frank's sweet voice—even his cry. Tell him to learn fast to talk. Tell Anna I must bring her a frock. Tell Will I will speak to Colonel Summers about the dog, and bring him a knife.

The Legislature adjourns next Monday week. I will be at home on Wednesday 17th, when it will give me pleasure to see you and the children once more.

I saw the Governor this evening. He requests an interview with me and the other members of the Legislature to-morrow, on the subject of * * * pardon. So much has been said about his pardoning *everybody* that he has become extremely cautious. I think, however, he will pardon him.

The Railroad Bill is going on finely. The State will take two-fifths of the stock.

I have not yet even seen to know Mr. Heyward. If I can make it convenient I will seek his acquaintance, but I see very little of the members of the House who do not board at Maybin's.

The death of Mr. Cleveland was expected. How many deaths happen in Greenville whilst I am absent. Colonel Dawkins was inquiring about Mr. Cleveland this morning. I have not yet seen his wife.

I must now conclude my letter, as my paper is pretty well filled and my topics exhausted, and it is late in the evening and I must put this letter in the office to-night.

Colonel Ware and Duncan and myself all received letters this morning from our better halves. Whether Walker did or not I do not know.

Yours truly,   B. F. PERRY.

COLUMBIA, Monday Night.

MY DEAR WIFE: I have only time to thank you for your letter Sunday evening. In obedience to your advice, I have written a *long* letter for the Mountaineer and therefore have no time to write you. You see what you get by your advice.

I have been all day to-day in the Court of Appeals, until 3 o'clock. Then I went to the Senate and staid there till 5. 1 have gained Kilgore's case in the Court of Appeals, and lost one I gained at Laurens. The other cases have not yet come on.

I hope you will receive to-morrow the box of fruits sent you and that it will be in time for your party. The night you wrote me, you must have received my letter informing you that the fruit was sent.

You ask about my clothes. They fit remarkably well, but I have done so much writing in them that I am afraid of wearing them out.

Mr. Elias Earle has just called and says he will go up in the morning. Colonel Ancrum was elected to-day. But for Maxwell's running, Earle might have been elected.

Tell Willie that Colonel Summer says he is going to write him a letter about the puppy. He has no puppy yet for him, but will have the next time. I will certainly bring the knife and will, as soon as I have leisure, write Willie a pretty letter.

Tell Anna that I will bring her something; but she has had so many dolls and breaks them so rapidly, I do not know so well about bringing a doll.

Tell Frank that a whip is easier brought than a drum and costs a good deal less. I will bring him a whip.

I wish to see you all very much and wish that I was going up with Major Earle, so that I might be there in time to be at your party. But no, I do not care to be at your party. I rather have the whole of your company to myself when I do return.

If you do not hear from me by the next mail you need not be surprised. And you will be so busy entertaining your company that you will not have time to read my letter. I hope you will have better weather than we now have. It has rained all day.

In my letter to Wells you will see an account of a debate we had in the Senate. I have tried to give quite a spirited sketch. You will see a compliment to the ladies and wives.

We all had an interview with the Governor about * * *

case last Saturday. He has given no answer yet. I think he intends granting a pardon.

I have seen nothing further of Alston Hayne. I suppose he has returned; nor have I been able to visit Taylor and Mrs. Martin, and probably will not before I leave.

I am glad your mother has received her money, and hope she will immediately pay Colonel Hoke.

I must conclude this hasty scrawl.

Yours truly and affectionately,   B. F. PERRY.

P. S.: In your next letter, I shall look out for a scold about the books.

COLUMBIA, S. C., Wednesday Night.

MY DEAR LIZ: It is now near 11 o'clock and I have just returned from the Senate. You must expect only a few lines. From 10 to 3 I was engaged in court. From then I have been engaged in the Senate till 10, with the exception of time to get dinner.

I was disappointed last stage by Mr. Earle. He says he is going in the morning and will carry this letter. Thomas Butler is here also, and William Rowland, but they will not go till the next stage.

Your very welcome letter was received this evening, enclosing Susan's note. I do not wish you to postpone your party on my account. I had rather you should have it before my return; but if you see proper to postpone it until after I reach home it will make no difference with me.

Your letter did not scold me as much as I expected about the purchase of books. I hope before this time you have received your fruit. The grapes are nice and delicious.

I shall no doubt surprise you when I inform you that I am a Candidate. The joint committee to nominate Trustees of the South Carolina College has put my name down amongst them. The Legislature has to vote on it to-morrow. This was done without my knowledge. It is considered a high honor. Dr. Gibbes, Colonel Goodwin, General Caldwell and Colonel McCord have all been electioneering for it the whole session and ar disappointed. They have not been nominated, whilst I have been, who never thought of it and was greatly surprised when I heard of the nomination. The Board of Trustees consists of the most distinguished men in the State.

I have no time to write you about our Legislature. I should be glad to hear Frank talk a little to-night. I hope Will has received his letter. Tell Anna if I had time I would write her one.

Mr. Walker has been sick for three days past, but is better. I have heard nothing further from the Governor.

Mr. Elias Earle has been in my room and just left and it is now near 12 o'clock in the night, so I must bid you good-night, my dear wife. B. F. PERRY.

COLUMBIA, S. C., Saturday Morning.

MY DEAR LIZ: I have but a few moments to write you by Mr. Butler. Last night it was 12 o'clock when I got my supper, on my return from the State House. For the last three nights we have sat until near 11 o'clock.

I received your letter last evening, and was glad to hear you were all well, and that your party was to take place after my return; but in postponing it you may disappoint Mr. McBee's friend's from North Carolina, which you ought not to do. Edmund Rhett took dinner with us the other day and inquired kindly about you and your mother. He told me some anecdotes about you all and Mrs. Potter, in New Haven. He seemed astonished when I told him Susan had been married while I was in Columbia. He said he thought she had determined not to marry.

I will endeavor to bring the little presents you name, but I shall hardly have time to get them. Indeed, I have no time to do anything, not even to go and see Mrs. Taylor and Mrs. Martin.

For several days past we have had some hard discussions in the Senate in which I have taken a part. The alteration of the circuits has taken place again. Mr. Ward, of Georgetown, said to me he wished me to be a Judge some day, and did not wish me to have to come to Georgetown so early as the court now sits. I was elected a Trustee of the College yesterday.

I was one of a special committee on the Beaufort College. Mr. Robert Barnwell sent for me in court to talk about the college and the business before the committee. I was much pleased with him. He afterwards appeared before the committee and made a speech, and an admirable one it was.

I shall be at home Wednesday night. We are all well. Kiss the children for me.   Your affectionate husband,

                                        B. F. PERRY.

ANDERSON, C. H., Wednesday Morning.

MY DEAR WIFE: I thank you for your note by Colonel Townes, and was pleased to have so good an account of Susan's situation at the Factory.

I have been reading the prose works of Mrs. Ellis on "Women, Daughters, Wives and Mothers." It is a most admirable book. I must purchase it whenever I can, and read it to you. I am sure you would be delighted with it.

The weather has been very bad ever since I have been here. I am afraid very little has yet been done on my farm. It has now cleared off and I hope Jim will proceed rapidly with the planting.

I have not heard anything from my mother, and I am very much afraid that I shall not have time to go by her house on my way to Pickens. The prospect now is that I shall be detained here till Saturday evening. No case has yet been tried in which I am concerned.

I have nothing to write you, except to say how glad I should be to be at home this bright morning, with you and the children. I hope the little creatures are *merry* this morning, without being too *musical*. There is no pleasure in life so agreeable to a correct mind and a warm heart as that which we derive from being at home with those we love.

I hope you will write me by Saturday's mail, which leaves Friday night; but you must certainly write me by some one going to Pickens next Sunday.

                    Yours truly and devotedly,   B. F. PERRY.

ANDERSON C. H., Thursday Night.

MY DEAR WIFE: I have just left the company below for the purpose of writing you a few lines by the stage in the morning.

I thank you for your letter this morning. It gave me great pleasure to hear you were all well. I was truly sorry to hear Will had been under the necessity of taking medicine. I hope it has been of permanent advantage to him. Anna and Frank are well, I trust. * * * *

I should like to hear from the farm and know how Jim and Charles are doing; but I am very much afraid I shall not be able to return home before Pickens court. My slander case will not be reached before to-morrow evening and we cannot finish it before Saturday. If I do not return, I shall go by Mr. Calhoun's and see his farm and take some lessons from it. I will also visit Colonel John Ewing Colhoun, and perhaps stay there Saturday night.

I have exchanged my guard chain. I saw Joe Powell have one which looked like it, thought it was brass. Storle got it of Miss Jones and sold it for $3. I have also exchanged my breast pin for a beautiful *brilliant*—the prettiest little thing of the kind you ever saw, price $22. I have bought as a present for you, or rather taken in exchange for my chain, a pair of beautiful silver butter knives, which you need very much. I have also a present for you of two silver mustard spoons, and the fellow still owes me $3.62. For it I had thought of getting a pair of gold sleeve buttons for Will. I intended to take a gold pen for you, but he has but one, and that is injured. I have now a silk guard chain. General Thompson promised me that Eliza should make me one if I would sell the gold one, which he says is not in good taste. I know you could make me one or lend me your gold chain to wear.

I have done a pretty good business here this court. I wish you would write to me at Pickens court by some one—Thompson, Townes or some one else. Let me hear all about the children, your noble self, Susan and McBee, the servants and the farm, the letters for me, etc.

If I do not return home, I shall not be able to see you before Sunday week. I have no hope of getting off from Pickens until Sunday. I ought to be at home to see about my business in the office. I should like to see my mother and brothers, but I shall not be able to go by and see them.

They are now talking so in my room that I must conclude by telling you good-night. Kiss the children for me, my dear Liz, and believe me,

Yours affectionately,   B. F. PERRY.

PICKENS C. H., Wednesday Night.

MY DEAR WIFE: I will write you a few lines by Mr. Speer, who returns to Greenville in the morning. Colonel Townes went this morning, but I had not time to write by him, and I had written the day before by Elford.

It would give me great satisfaction to be at home this evening with you and the children. It really seems to me almost an age since I have had that pleasure. The time seems longer from the fact that I have seen so many persons going from Anderson and Pickens to Greenville, and yet not able to go myself; but I have had some compensation for my absence, by the receipt of $520 in cash since I left home. I hope to pay Moore's debt at Greenville court, and relieve you of *that worriment.*

I have not yet tried any of my cases. Two will come on to-morrow and I hope to leave the next day. About this, however, I am altogether uncertain. Some of my most important cases have been continued.

I have had various solicitations to run for Congress. Many persons of influence in different parts of the district have said that they had selected me as the next candidate; but this is out of my power, and I do not think that Simpson will decline.

The weather is terrible. I hope it is better at Greenville. My cows and your house-cleaning do not go on so well, I imagine, whilst the rain is falling. The poor cows must suffer. This weather will kill a great many of them in the country. They cannot survive bad weather and a want of food.

The streets in Pickens are truly in a laughable condition. To walk them is almost impossible.

You must remember me kindly to Susan and McBee. I think of them very often, and hope they are, and will do, well. Your mother and Anne are often in my mind, likewise and also my poor mother, whose situation is deplorable, and yet she bears it with patience, fortitude and even cheerfulness. I have inherited much from her in this respect.

You must now kiss the children for me. I hope and *believe* they will *all* inherit our good sense and good principles. If they do, I shall be happy. All that I care for is to bring them up properly, teach them good habits and industry, and give them an education so they can support themselves.

I must now bid you good-night, my dear Liz.

Yours in love,   B. F. Perry.

Laurens C. H., Tuesday Night.

My Dear Liz: I am afraid, from the progress yet made in court, that I shall be detained here till Sunday. I have four cases of great importance and no prospect of reaching any of them before Thursday or Friday, and I cannot think of leaving until the last is disposed of.

I saw Mr. Cunningham here to-day. He was indicted in court for an assault and battery, but the case was compromised and he got off with a fine of one dollar. He informed me that Miss Pamela had been extremely ill, last week; that he had despaired of her living, but that she was now better. She was worse than she ever had been, and Dr. Arnold was sent for.

I will send you the Laurensville Herald, which contains my communication and the remarks of the editor. He has treated my explanation very fairly and published my speech. I am entirely satisfied with the result.

Judge Wardlaw is holding court here, and seems sad; no doubt mourning for the loss of his wife. I am pleased with Judge Wardlaw's notions about the government of slaves. They correspond with my own.

General Thompson is here, but is not going on to Washington until after the courts are over. He says he is very much disturbed about Butler's eye, and thinks he may lose the sight of it.

Mr. Cunningham told me there was no prospect of Ben Yancey's getting married.

I hope you are doing well in your garden and will have everything in nice order when I return. You had better plant such seeds as the season suits. Send and get a paper of carrots and parsnips and plant.

Tell Jim and March I wish to see a great deal done at the farm on my return. Let the ground all be broken up and ready for planting corn next week. Tell them that next week I wish to plant corn, and for them to have everything ready —carry out the manure.

Kiss the children for me and say to them that I forgot to to kiss them when I was starting, and that I have thought of the omission often. It would give me great pleasure to be with you all to-night, and hear them fret and cry in the morning. I do not know how much I love you all until I am absent from you.

It is now late in the night and I must go to bed. If I have time, I will write you by Friday's mail.

The prospects of the railroad are dull, but it is said that a good deal of stock will be taken in Laurens during the summer, and also in Newberry. I hear $100,000 have been taken in Charleston, but I am afraid it is too good news to be true.

My dear wife, good-night. Mr. Wells will leave in the morning for Greenville, and perhaps may carry this letter.

Yours truly and affectionately,   B. F. PERRY.

COLUMBIA, S. C., Friday Evening.

MY DEAR LIZ: I have just received your letter and was much gratified to hear you were all well. I had been invited by Colonel Wigfall to drink wine with himself and Colonel Manning, and left the table when the mail was opened, to get your letter. They insisted on my not going, but I said I expected to hear from "*my wife.*"

I have but a short time to write you, as I have to go down to the college immediately after tea to hear the senior class speak. I was there last night till eleven o'clock, and as a Trus-

tee occupied quite a conspicuous seat, amidst the professors
and judges, surrounded by a crowded gallery of ladies and
gentlemen. The students performed well, and the college is in
a most prosperous state.

I arrived here Wednesday evening, just in time to take my
seat at the board of Trustees, and we were kept sitting until
after 11 o'clock We meet again next Wednesday night. No
election of Bursar yet. There are about twenty candidates. I
had hardly got out of the stage when Dr. Davis called to electioneer with me. I told him I had to vote for Anderson, but if
he withdrew I would support him.

I have been to-day performing a duty imposed on Mr.
Withers, Colonel Manning and myself, as a committee of the
Board of Trustees, to report on the communications received
from the President and Professors. To-morrow night I am
invited by Colonel Preston to go 'round to his house and eat
strawberries. He wishes the Trustees to meet the senior class
at his house.

I have not yet, and I am afraid I will not, reach any of my
cases in the Court of Appeals, for a week or ten days. In fact
there is some danger of having to stay here till the last of the
month. But for my duty as Trustee I should return home and
come back again.

None of the lawyers from my circuit will be here before Monday. We will then determine what to do, whether to wait or
postpone our cases.

I came down all alone in the stage to Newberry. There I was
joined by Mr. Pope and two young men—one of them comes
down to be admitted to the Bar. Tom Lawrence Jones and Pettigru's son Daniel came up last night to apply. Jones looked
so plain I hardly knew him. He has cut off all his beard, and
laid aside his fine clothes, and looks like a different being. He
says I must give him a certificate of moral character, as he is
better acquainted with me than any other lawyer here. Pettigru's son does not seem promising.

I saw Perry Butler and delivered his letters and bundles.
The package to H. Thruston I sent by Colonel Summer, who
inquired for his little friend as soon as he spoke to me. He
seems to have been very much taken with Willie. General Bon-

ham inquired after you all. He seems very happy and talks about his anxiety to get back home again.

I will write you again on Monday next. Tell Jim as soon as he has finished replanting to plant the new ground, and sow the herds grass in the wet places, where it is too wet for corn.

I will execute all your commissions contained in your letter. Tell Will I will bring him the ball, etc. If Will goes to school again, make him come home at 12 o'clock. Take care of yourself, and the children, my dear wife.

B. F. PERRY.

COLUMBIA, S. C., Monday Morning.

MY DEAR LIZ: I will write you a few lines this morning before the court meets. I am afraid I shall not not have time to do so after the adjournment of court.

We arrived here yesterday evening about 3 o'clock, very tired and dusty—Judge Earle, Colonel Townes, Edward Earle and Mr. Young. We made free use of your breadstuffs on the road and they were very much praised, and also you yourself was praised by all for being so good and kind a wife in providing for her husband so bountifully. Judge Earle thought the corn pound cake exceedingly good and could hardly believe that it was all corn meal.

I have just been to the court to look at the docket, and find a great many cases ahead of mine. I am afraid of being detained here until the last of next week.

I saw Judge Evans this morning, who inquired after you. Mr. Pendleton is here and inquired kindly after you. Not many of the lawyers have yet got in. Mr. Pendleton has got a good many subscribers to his paper. I have given him my revolutionary incidents and he seemed very thankful for them. He asked if he might state by whom they were written. They will therefore appear as written by me.

I have bought "Zanoni," but the other books you wish cannot be had. I have bought a new novel by Sims, of Darlington, a member of the Legislature, whom you may have heard me speak of as a young man of talent. It is dedicated to Judge Evans. The style is good. It is a tale of the Revolution, called " Bevil Faulcon."

There was a great to-do here the other day about four students who went off to Texas without the knowledge of their parents. They were from Camden. One was a son of Colonel McWillie, whom you have heard me speak of. There was a great crowd assembled to see them start. The professors in college came down and tried to restrain them. They went off in the stage, and it will be very mortifying to their parents.

I went yesterday evening to look at the burnt part of the town. It is sad to behold. I met there Dr. Blanding. He told me that Mrs. McRae had been brought home, and that there was little or no hope of her son's recovery. He is still in the asylum.

My pen is so bad and the ink has grease in it, that it pains me to write. I hope to hear from you Wednesday. I hope you are getting on well with the house and servants and that the children are all well. The dear little creatures, how I could kiss and squeeze them this morning! There is no place like home, and there are no persons whose company gives us such pleasure as the members of one's family. You and the children are to me everything in this world, and always with you I could be happy.

My pen is so bad and cannot be mended, I must conclude. Give my love to your mother and sisters and believe me,

Your devoted husband,   B. F. PERRY.

COLUMBIA, S. C., May 12th, 1846.

MY DEAR WIFE: I received no letter from you by Sunday's mail. I shall anxiously expect one by the next mail.

It is more than likely that I may return home next Friday evening. There is no hope of reaching my cases under two or three weeks. Young, Whitner, Sullivan, Irby and Orr are now here, and we will probably make an arrangement to-morrow to continue all of our cases and go home. Whitner has his wife with him and Mrs. Mays is to be here to-night. Harrison is here with his wife. General Thompson came here yesterday and says Cornelia Crittenden will also be here to-night. She stopped a day in Orangeburg with her cousin, John Cunningham, and all the Abbeville lawyers came in to-day and yesterday. We now have quite a gathering.

There was quite a pleasant party at Colonel Preston's Saturday evening. I met Mrs. Ellet again. She invited me to her soiree Wednesday evening, but the Board of Trustees meet that evening. Withers, Manning and myself have been busy about the college every day.

The students for admission to the Bar are examined next Wednesday and I am on the committee again. Have just prepared my questions. Fortunately, I brought my old ones down with me. There are some fifteen making application.

I purchased the works of Hugh S. Legare, and was not a little surprised to learn from Colonel Wigfall that *I* was mentioned in them: that my name had reached Brussels! I have been reading the work with some interest. He is very severe on the Nullifiers.

I was at church on Sunday and heard Mr. Thornwell preach a fine sermon. I saw Chancellor Harper at Colonel Preston's. His health is desperate and he cannot live long. He inquired about Anne and your mother.

I have bought your knives and a carving knife and fork, a ball for Willie that will bounce as high as the house. No hat as yet. Price same as in Greenville—$1.50, and Panama $3.

I hope you are not much alarmed about the war. There is great interest felt here to know more about it. We shall hear in a few days.

I saw Pringle here on Saturday. Mr. Poinsett will be here to-night.

Colonel Irby brings me news that you have had a great deal of rain in Greenville and I am afraid my crop is all ruined and the land all washed away.

In my last letter I said nothing about being anxious to get back home. You once told me not to write so much about that. I will not, at *present*, but only leave you to imagine how much pleasure it would give me to see you and the children. The remembrance of home is always a delightful one. I forget that the children ever cry or behave badly.

I saw at Colonel Preston's a beautiful marble bust of Mrs. Preston, by Powers. It is worth looking at, and made me ashamed of my plaster of paris busts. He has a great many fine paintings. His library was on shelves in the dining-room, but not so large as mine.

My dear Liz, good-night. If I do not return home by the next stage I will write you. Kiss the children for me and believe me, Yours truly, etc , B. F. PERRY.

COLUMBIA, S. C., Wednesday Evening.

My DEAR WIFE: I have just received your letter written on Monday, and am greatly surprised that you did not hear from me on Sunday evening. I wrote you a long letter and sent it to the postoffice. I hope you have received that and another written on Monday night, before this time.

I was glad to hear you and the children were all well, but sorry to hear of the quarrelling of Jim and Maria. I hope they will do better. They are getting *seasoned* to each other's badness. I suppose all married people, black and white, have some scrapes, except our noble selves. But I believe negroes are generally happier living apart. I will arrange it all when I come home.

I was much provoked yesterday about my passage in the stage to Greenville. Dr. King has engaged the whole stage for to-morrow morning. I paid at Greenville for my passage back. and claimed my right; but to-day I found that Mr. Young desired my services in a case to-morrow, in a case before Judge Wardlaw, and I must stay till the next stage. So this will settle all difficulties about my passage and Dr. King, but I shall be two days longer without seeing you. My seat for Saturday is taken and General Thompson, Young and Jones have all taken seats in the same stage. I shall be at home Sunday night, but none of my cases reached—all postponed till next fall.

To-day I assisted in examining the students. They were all admitted. To-night I meet the Board of Trustees, and if off in time, we will all go to Mrs. Ellett's *soiree*, which I understand will be a very magnificent affair—a sort of Fair for the benefit of the orphans of Columbia, in which the ladies generally have united There is great preparation in the way of roses and ice cream, as I have discovered to-day, in passing the streets.

You may tell Mr. McBee's family that I wrote a decree to-day for Judge Johnson to sign in favor of Mr. McBee, about the gold mine, and will bring it up with me.

I received a letter from Mr. Peroneau and another from Mr. Petigru yesterday, in favor of Wilbur as Bursar.

I have not yet purchased Willie's hat. There are no pretty ones. They seem to have no hats for boys except mean straw ones at fifty cents. I may find one yet. I have bought the india rubber and the ball. The doll and the whip I will get. I have bought a shot-gun, for shooting hawks, squirrels, etc., a very pretty gun, for $12. The price was $15. Also a pair of boots, at $9. My shoes would not answer for the mud. I have bought only two or three law books.

I am sorry to hear about the rain. It has been wet here and is now very hot. I am anxious to get home, and when I heard Dr. King had got the whole stage to himself I was much provoked. Nothing did or could have reconciled me but business.

I have not yet seen Mrs. Whitner and Mrs. Mays. They go up to-morrow morning.

I must now close my letter and carry it to the postoffice, before I go to the college. Kiss the children for me.

Your affectionate husband,   B. F. PERRY.

COLUMBIA COURT HOUSE, June, 1844, }
Monday 3 o'clock. }

MY DEAR LIZ: I only have time to write you a word or two. I have been so much engaged that I could not write you by last mail, and it is the same thing now.

Your first letter gave me great pleasure, but your last one was sad enough in every way. Poor Judge Earle. We had a meeting of the bar this morning, at the request of the Judges. Colonel Preston was called to the chair and I offered some

Resolutions, which you will see in the papers. I made a biographical speech to the Court of Appeals on Judge Earle and Judge Johnson replied. The speeches will also be published.

It is possible I may start home in the morning. If so I shall be with you, my dear wife and my dear little children, on Thursday night. God knows it will be to me a source of great happiness and pleasure.

I have much to write you, but no time to do it in, as the mail is closing.

Kiss the children for me and tell them I have a great many presents for them.　　　　Yours truly and lovingly,

B. F. PERRY.

COLUMBIA, S. C., July 3d, 1846.

MY DEAR WIFE: Although I have just started on my tour, only one night from home, and yet I am disposed to avail myself of an opportunity of writing to you. In fact you and the children have scarcely been out of my mind for ten minutes since I left home. I regret that I have not all of you with me. The conduct of Will, the night I started, in running down the stair case to kiss and hug me once more before I departed, deeply affected me. He has an affectionate heart. He will one day make a man of some figure in the world, I hope. Anna is so kind and affectionate, so much like my old mother, and being a daughter, is my favorite. Little Frank is a noble fellow, and how I wish I had him on my knees this evening, by your bedside. But I have left you all in the care of your mother, and I am sure, feel certain that you will be well taken care of. It is said that a mother's love is the strongest feeling of human nature, and I know your mother possesses it in its greatest strength. But I think a husband's love for his wife, and the mother of his children, as strong as any human feeling need be.

I had a pleasant trip down here—the stage all alone to myself and my journey had been preceded with most refreshing and delightful showers, which laid the dust and cooled the atmosphere. In the lower part of Laurens I heard of much sickness, and some deaths from fevers, whereupon I took out Dr.

Crook's pills and swallowed them without water or anything
else to facilitate their downward course. I never felt better
than I do. I weighed at Colonel McNeely's 192 pounds. He
said he wanted to see how much I would gain in my travels:
says I will weigh at least 200 when I return.

I hope you have had rains since I left home. Tell Jim he
must continue to harrow the corn until it is all silking. Crops
look fine on the road and the corn made is out of danger from
droughts, etc.

At Newberry I sent for Colonel Fair. He was at Edgefield
court, but I heard that he and Patrick Caldwell and Mr.
Nance were all going on to the North next Tuesday. I am
afraid the news is too good to be true. How I would like to
have Colonel Fair as a traveling companion. He is a noble-
hearted fellow and I love him much.

You must return my thanks to Mr. Poinsett, Mrs. Butler
and your mother for the letters they gave me, although I may
not be able to deliver one-fourth of them. My journey is more
to look at the country than to become acquainted with people.

Should you see any of Tom Butler's family, you may tell
them I think there is but little doubt of his election as Major.
I have heard from all the companies but Chester, and he is
thirty votes ahead of Major Gladden, the next highest candidate.

I have seen no one scarcely since I reached Columbia. Ate
dinner, washed, dressed and sat down to write you this letter.
Nothing to write about, either, so I commenced praising our
children and speaking of a husband's love—old themes, but
nevertheless interesting ones. You, however, have had too
many proofs of my love in actions and conduct to have it
strengthened by words. Your sweetness and womanly soft-
ness have too often made my sternness and inflexibility of
purpose yield to your own wishes, to doubt your influence
over me. I was not born to obey, and yet you almost always
make me yield to your feelings and wishes.

But enough. Remember me to your mother, Susan and
Anne. Susan, I suppose, begins to feel a young mother's love.
I hope she may be as happy in life as her disinterested affec-

tion through life merits. And I pray that Anne, too, may be restored to health and happiness. Her fate has, indeed, been a sad one. Your affectionate husband,

B. F. PERRY.

WASHINGTON, D. C., July 6th, 1846.

MY DEAR WIFE: I arrived in this city yesterday evening and have not yet recovered from the excessive fatigue of the journey. I will, however, endeavor to give you a brief account of my travels so far.

The morning after I wrote you in Columbia, I set out on the railroad for Charleston, in company with Professor Henry, of the South Carolina College. I had quite a *tete-a-tete* with him as far as Branchville; he then turned up for Aiken. The downward cars had Judge Dunkin on board, but I did not find it out till we had landed in Charleston. He inquired after you very particularly. I saw no one in Charleston. The boat started at 4 o'clock. We had a crowd on board. In the night a most terrible storm overtook us, and I asssure you I never spent a more wretched night. We were in great danger from the wind and lightning. I slept none. It was excessively hot, and we had to close all the windows to keep the rain and water out. The heat broke out all over my body, and in many places the skin is as red as blood. Sunday morning we landed in Wilmington and took the cars for Weldon, where we arrived at night—160 miles. Travelled all night; came to Petersburg about sunrise, ate breakfast at Richmond and arrived here at 5 o'clock. I took lodgings at the National Hotel, a very splendid building. Almost the first man I saw was General Thompson. He was glad to see me and hear from home. I next saw Frederick Rutledge, then a Mr. Mikell from near Beaufort. He was going round to Burt's to take tea. After tea Burt and Yancey come to see me and we sat and talked till near 10 o'clock. In the meantime I met my old acquaintance, General Rusk, of Texas. General Thompson called up Commodore Morris and introduced me to him, and I informed him Mr. Poinsett had given me a letter to him. He in-

quired very kindly about Mr. Poinsett and invited General
Thompson and myself to call and see him.

In the morning I went down to the Capitol. It is a magnificent building and greatly surpassed my expectations for
grandeur and beauty. The grounds, too, are magnificent. I
was introduced into the House by Mr. Yancey. Simpson came
over to see me. So did Rhett and Holmes, Black, Woodward
and Burt. I was greatly astonished at the appearance of the
members. They are, indeed, a most inferior looking set of
men; seem to have very little talent, and one-half of them
look like they had no pretentions to be called gentlemen. I
was more shocked at their rudeness and vulgarity than I was
at their bad looks. They are a rowdy set, and nothing could
induce me to be a member of that House. I went with General
Thompson into the Senate. He introduced me to Crittenden,
of Kentucky; Lewis of Alabama; Barrow, of Louisiana, and
Archer, of Virginia. The latter invited me to take tea with
him to-morrow evening. I spoke to Mr. Calhoun, but I did not
see McDuffie. Colonel Benton is decidedly the most striking
and imposing man I have seen. I am to go to his house to
deliver my letter. The Vice-President, Mr. King, is also strikingly aristocratic in appearance. A good many of the Senators are inferior looking.

I have engaged some clothes, but they will not be ready for
some days and will detain me here, otherwise I should go
North immediately.

I hope to hear from you before I leave this city. I shall endeavor to write a letter for the Mountaineer, but really the
breaking out of the heat annoys me so at night that I am almost crazy. I commenced writing this letter last night, but
had to stop on that account.

I feel as if I was a long ways from home, and am anxious
to see you and the children. It seems to me that I have been
from home a month, at least.

You must excuse this hasty scrawl. I will write you again
before I leave Washington. Kiss the children and give my
love to your mother and family.

Yours etc.,   B. F. PERRY.

SANS-SOUCI.

WASHINGTON, July 10th, 1846.

MY DEAR WIFE: The weather is so dreadfully hot I can hardly muster courage enough to write you. It has been one week since I left home, and really to me it seems like an age. I have traveled so far and seen so much that it seems impossible that I have done all this in one week. I hope you and the children are all well and that I shall receive a letter shortly saying so. I left you unwell, and when I think of it, I am almost ashamed of my conduct; but you were willing and persuaded me to come.

I have just written a letter to Colonel Townes, giving a full account of what I have seen and noticed. To that letter I refer, and you must consider it a part and parcel of this.

I had the pleasure of going to the President's yesterday evening, and was charmed with Mrs. Polk. There was an immense crowd of persons in the grounds around the building. The President is not so prepossessing in his manners as his wife. I saw and was introduced to another fine lady, Mrs. Crittenden, of Kentucky. Yesterday I spent at Archer's, in company with the Russian Minister, Barrow, Senator from Louisiana; Crittenden, of Kentucky; General Thompson, and Pendleton, of Virginia. I called to see Commodore Morris, General Towson, Major Cooper and Colonel Benton. Commodore Morris returned my visit this morning, Holmes, Woodward, Simpson and Black, all called to see me this morning and left their cards. Mr. Critttenden also did me the honor to call and leave his card. I dined with Simpson to-day. General Towson seemed very glad to hear from Mrs. Butler, and requested me to call and see Mrs. Towson. Major Cooper seemed delighted to hear from Mr. and Mrs. Poinsett. Colonel Benton was not at home. I saw Mrs. Benton and her three daughters, one of them married to Colonel Fremont, of the army. When I gave Mrs. Fremont the letter from Poinsett, she said she was entitled to one-half the letters her father received from him. They seemed quite a pleasant and agreeable family; not pretty but not ugly, healthy and rosy cheeked. General Thompson went with me, and he has been very kind to me. I feel under many obligations to him for his politeness. It has been of great service to me.

I was delighted with Barrow, of Louisiana. He is a noble looking man, and, I think, a noble hearted fellow with handsome talents. I have yet seen very few pretty women. They do not strike me at all. Mr. Calhoun came up to me to-day and seemed very kind. I have not seen McDuffie. Yancey's mother is here and has fallen out with Cunningham's family and Ben. Mrs. Calhoun and Mrs. Burt left here this morning for the Virginia springs.

Commodore Shubrick is in command of the navy yard at this place. I went to visit the yard and did not carry your mother's letter with me, nor did I see him. I will send it to him. Barnwell Rhett seems very kind and clever.

I have just got my clothes—coat, pantaloons and three vests—$45.50. They fit very well, and if I had my shirts I should look quite genteel.

I shall not leave here before next Sunday. You must write me in Boston how you are coming on, and the children and the farm, etc.; how Willie learns, what they say, etc.; what sort of a present they wish, etc. Barrow told me the other night he wished to have twenty-five sons—that he would rather have a distinguished son than to be distinguished himself. I told him I expected Mrs. Barrow would object to the number, which made him smile. He is a noble gentleman. Good-night.   Your affectionate husband,

                                             B. F. PERRY.

WASHINGTON, July 12th, 1845.

MY DEAR WIFE: I will write you a few lines this morning before breakfast. I am not in such a rack of pain as I was when I wrote you last. But the weather is the hottest I have ever felt. Last night I went to the President's alone. Burt was to have gone with me. I first rode to Mr. Calhoun's, where I spent a few minutes very pleasantly with him. I had some apprehensions in going to the White House alone, for fear I would not be recognized. There was a great crowd assembled. I pushed my way through to the President and then to Mrs. Polk, who said, in her kind manner, "How do you do, Mr. Perry?" I entered into conversation with her. She expressed great astonishment that I had never been to Washington before; said she could hardly believe it. We spoke of South Carolina, the mountains, Tennessee, the French Broad, down which she had once travelled, the Hudson, etc.

I met Colonel Benton at the President's and had a long talk with him about Oregon and his speech. I complimented it very highly and he seemed pleased. I understand he is very greedy of praise and flattery and does not hesitate to talk of himself. The President was near by and heard my compliments, which he did not seem to relish, as it was rather a censure on him, as he differed widely from Colonel Benton. I noticed he turned off and sat down. I was introduced to Colonel Benton in the Senate Chamber yesterday, by Mr. Yancey. He told me that Benton would speak of his daughters, who were educated by himself, in very high terms. He said, "Sir, my daughters are well educated. They are capable of conversing, with ease, with the crowned heads of Europe!!!" Mrs. Fremont, it is said, possesses all of her father's talents, and I should suppose so from what I saw of her.

Mr. Yancey has resigned his seat in Congress; is going to move to Montgomery to practice law in co-partnership with Elmore, of that place.

I dined with Mr. Simpson the other day. He lives by himself—only one other member of Congress with him. He has been very kind to me. And General Thompson—I feel under a thousand obligations to him. I have become acquainted with Governor Bagby, of Alabama, through Mr. Yancey. I was also introduced to Yulee and Westcot, of Florida. I saw Mrs. Yulee last night at the President's. She is very pretty.

Yesterday I heard a debate in the Senate between Calhoun, Webster, Dix of New York; Davis, of Massachusetts; Archer, of Virginia. I also heard Benton speak on another subject. I liked Calhoun's style of speaking more than that of any other. I felt proud of him. He sent me his report the other day on the Memphis Convention, and yesterday he came to me in the Senate Chamber and asked if I had read it, and I had hardly looked over it. He asked me what I thought of it, and begged me to write something in the Mountaineer about the subject, in order to call the attention of our friends to it. This placed me in a most delicate situation, as I differ with him in some respects. I told him I would think of it.

If I do not stop, my letter will not be at the post office by 8 o'clock, when the mail closes. I hope to hear from you on Monday. Tuesday I will go North. Mr. Yancey speaks of going with me. Kiss the children a dozen times for me, my dear Liz. Your affectionate husband,

B. F. PERRY.

WASHINGTON, July 12th, 1846.

MY DEAR WIFE: I received your letter yesterday morning and was delighted to hear from home. I went to the post office to put in the letter I wrote you, and came very near coming off without inquiring for letters, not supposing you had had time to write me. I assure you it affords me great pleasure to receive a letter from my home and my dear wife, in a strange place. I hope, indeed, to meet you in blooming health; and it seems to me that we shall have been separated so long that our meeting will be like a second marriage. I am glad to hear Will is head; and that Frank missed me so much. I hope they will all be good children and grow better by my return, and I will bring them some pretty presents.

Yesterday I went to see Commodore Shubrick. He now lives in Washington and has command of the navy yard. He made a great many inquiries about your mother and family, and seemed very kind; sent for his daughter to come down and · see me, and introduced me as the husband of her cousin, Elizabeth McCall. Said he would call and see me, etc. His standing in the navy is very high, and he goes to sea in a few weeks.

From Commodore Shubrick's I went to the Capitol and was there introduced again to John Q. Adams, who I find represents the district in which my father was born. He invited me to call and see him and he would give me some information about my *name*. I had considerable conversation with him. He looks very much like my father, and I was so forcibly reminded of the likeness on first seeing him that I could not refrain from shedding tears. I never will say aught against him again, for I hold it imposssible for any one with his features to be a bad man.

I went into the Senate and there met for the first time Mr. McDuffie, who seemed very kind and invited me to take tea with him. I was introduced to Ritchie, the venerable editor of the Union. He inquired if I was Major Perry, of Greenville, S. C., and on being told yes, he replied: "You are a much stouter man than I expected to see. I had always formed an opinion that you were a small man." I had a long and very agreeable conversation with him.

In the evening Burt and myself took a ride and went to the walks of the Capitol, where some hundreds of ladies and gentelmen assemble every evening to hear the band of music, promenade, etc. I there met Miss * * I tried to avoid her, but she literally ran after me—begged me to call and see her. I found her with a member of Congress from Kentucky, but she is here alone, without any protector. I met Mrs. Woodward and walked over the ground with her and her husband and a Miss Camp, from New York. I met and was introduced to Mr. Winthrop, of Massachusetts, who is a *gentleman*. About dusk we returned to Mr. Calhoun's and took tea with Mr. McDuffie and Mr. Calhoun. After tea Middleton came in who married a Van Ness. I had met him in the Library in the morning and had a good deal of conversation with him after an introduction by Burt.

After sitting awhile, Burt and myself came to the hotel, where we found Colonel Fair and Mr. Nance, who had just arrived. I am delighted to have Colonel Fair for my travelling companion. He will detain me a day or two longer in Washington.

At the bar I found a letter from Colonel Totten inviting me to dine with him on Monday at 5 o'clock. He had just received a letter from Mr. Poinsett. I find Mr. Poinsett's friends very much attached to him here, and I could not have brought letters from a better source.

You can have no conception of the heat of the weather. It is actually purgatory. Such distress and complaint I never heard before. My room is surrounded by ladies, and such doleful lamentations do I hear!

You need be under no apprehensions about my money. I believe my trunk the safest place. Captain Rivers is here with his daughter, going North, and Mr. Bryce, of Columbia.

Adieu, my dear wife. My love to the children and your mother and family.   Your loving husband,

                                        B. F. PERRY.

                              WASHINGTON, July 13th, 1846.

MY DEAR WIFE: I write you this morning because I may not have an opportunity of writing you again for some days. The great Tariff debate in the Senate commences to-day, and from what I hear will continue several days. This may detain me in Washington, as it will be of great interest. The great men of the Senate will all take a part.

Yesterday was Sunday, and it was so hot that I did not go to church. I wrote you a letter in the morning. After breakfast I pulled off my clothes and lay on my bed pretty much till dinner, thinking of you and the children. I always thought, when with you and the children, that I loved you all as much as it was possible for a husband and father to love his wife and family. But I never realized the full strength of my love till separated from you in a strange city, and no hope of seeing you for weeks to come. I thought to myself all day yesterday how little I appreciated, whilst at home, the value and the pleasure of yours and the children's company, and how much I would value it on my return.

In the evening I went with General Thompson, by appointment, to see Webster. We found him sitting on his front portico, with his coat and waistcoat off. He looked as plain as any old farmer or country magistrate. He said to me: "I have heard of you before." I told him that I once had the pleasure of receiving a letter from him. He ordered some claret, whisky and water. I and General Thompson drank of the claret and water. He drank whiskey and water. He spoke of the Tariff, Mr. Calhoun, internal improvements, Oregon, the Mexican war, the character of the American people, agriculture, England, stock, Tallyrand, France, etc. I enjoyed the conversation very much and was delighted with his simplicity and greatness. When I went to start, he asked me how long I would remain in the city. He asked me if he could do anything for me in Boston by way of letters, etc. Said he would send me to a gentleman near where my father was born, who would give me more information than I had any conception of, in regard to my name and myself.

From Webster's we went to Judge Mason's, Attorney General of the United States, and spent an hour or two very pleasantly with the Judge and his wife and children. Judge Mason is regarded as the purest and best man in Washington. His wife is pleasant and agreeable.

A good many South Carolinians are now here, and Judge Butler is to be here in a few days. I tell you, in great confidence, what you must not mention: That Governor Butler and Colonel Mason, of the army, are to fight a duel as soon as he arrives in Washington. This brings Judge Butler here. I have my information from General Thompson. But do not let it get out, as it would distress his family and friends. It is an old quarrel and cannot be made up.

Major Stark, of Hamburgh, is here, and also Mr. Bryce, of Columbia. They are all going North. So I shall have company enough.

To-day I must return some calls and visit old John Q. Adams, by appointment.

The weather is alarmingly hot, and it is truly distressing.

Breakfast is ready and I must conclude this letter. You may not hear from me again before I leave the city. I shall go to Baltimore and stay a day, thence to Philadelphia, New York, West Point, Albany, etc. Give my love to your mother, Susan, McBee and Anne. Kiss the children and accept the assurance of my love.

B. F. Perry.

Washington, July 15, 1846.

My Dear Wife: I received your second letter last night. I sent two or three times before I could get it. Once or twice the bar keeper told me there were no letters. I *knew* you had written me, and I leave here to-day. I was unwilling to start without hearing from you. General Thompson received letters from Mrs. Thompson and Butler, who sent word that all of my family were well, but I persevered until the letter came, and I was much gratified to hear you were all well. I shall now leave the city without regret, hoping to hear from you in New York and Boston.

I have not much to write about in addition to my last. I dined at Colonel Totten's Monday and was delighted with him and his family. He is a very intelligent and warm hearted gentleman, his wife is a most agreeable lady; his daughter is a sweet young lady. They all came up and shook hands with me and treated me as one of the family. He has two sons not grown. I believe he has one or two sons and daughters married whom I did not see. They all seem greatly attached to Mr. Poinsett.

Yesterday evening I went to the President's, in company with Burt, Simpson, Judge Butler and Fair. I told Mrs Polk that I had written Mrs. Perry some admirable sketches of the White House and its inmates, and assured her that the feeling of South Carolina was quite *loyal* that evening. Judge Butler, who was standing with me, said I should use the word "allegiance." Mrs. Polk replied that the other was the feeling when applied to a lady. We talked with her some time until a crowd came up and pushed us off. She is a most charming woman, and seems so happy at being Mrs. President. I don't think I ever saw a happier woman in my life. She has a little spice of vanity in her character and her heart is filled to overflowing with the idea of being the wife of the President, and she seems to look upon him as being worthy of all honor and admiration. I could but think how she would differ in opinion with those who called Mr. Polk a third rate man during the Presidential canvass. In her opinion he is first of the greatest. I will have a great deal to tell you about persons in Washington, but cannot write all.

I have written a letter to the Mountaineer, and in it mentioned my visit to Adams and the debate in the Senate. You will read that letter, and I will not repeat what is in it.

Judge Butler stays here a short time and returns to South

Carolina. Governor Butler has not yet arrived. Dr. May, who was once at Greenville, with Powell McRae, called to see me, yesterday. I also went by myself to see Crittenden, of Kentucky, and Archer, Senator from Virginia. I found them both very kind and pleasant. Yesterday I dined with Mr. Burt, at Calhoun's and McDuffie's in company with those gentlemen, Judge Butler, Simpson, Fair and Tucker, of Virginia. We had quite a pleasant party.

Colonel Fair and myself will start to-day for Baltimore. You will not hear from me for some days. I have not written yet to any one but you and Colonel Townes. I must write to some others when I get time.

My dear wife, you must take good care of yourself and children. Give my love to your mother and family and write me all the news. Write to Boston. My present plan is to go to New York, Saratoga, Niagara, down the river to Montreal and Quebec and back to Boston. Mr. Adams directed me to take this route and gave me all the particulars.

In great haste, yours truly

B. F. Perry.

PHILADELPHIA, July 18th, 1846.

MY DEAR WIFE: I have just written a long letter to Colonel Townes, describing everything I have seen since I left Washington, and to that letter I refer you.

I am now traveling with Colonel Fair. Yancey did not come on with us as we hoped. We will go on rapidly together till we reach Boston. There Colonel Fair will leave me and return home. I will stop along to deliver my letters and see more of the country. He will go with me to Niagara and Quebec. I find it very pleasant to have a friend with me, and will more so when I get into Canada.

I hope to hear from you in New York. If you write me within three or four days after you wrote me last in Washington, I shall receive it; but my stay will be a very short one in New York until my return.

In looking over Sully's Gallery of Paintings, I was struck with the painting of Adam and Eve. It is the most lovely picture ever saw, and if I had money would purchase it at $150. You will see some account of it in my letter to the Mountaineer. I am delighted with Philadelphia, but have seen no one. Your mother's letters I shall have to leave in the postoffice. I left Mrs. Heyward's at Wilmington, as I passed through it. I feel awkward in calling to see strange ladies, and I suppose they have some such feeling themselves. Nor shall I be able to call and see your uncle, Captain McCall, as I pass through New Jersey.

I was looking at some bracelets for you this morning. They are fashionable—one only—but I will take your advice, and make my purchases when I return. I saw a bedstead worth $2,500, a wardrobe $1,500, and the whole set for one chamber worth $8,000! I saw some beautiful and new fashioned sofas, French, price $150; some neat plain ones at $35.

I have met in Philadelphia Dr. Thompson, son of Wallace Thompson, of Union, who is attending the medical lectures. He has been very kind in showing us the city. I find hack hire costs me a great deal. They charge one dollar per hour for driving. In Washington my carriage hire amounted to almost as much as my board bill

So far, my dear wife, I have been delighted with my trip. I knew so little and had seen so little of the world before, compared with other gentlemen. I have learnt much and acquired much valuable information, which I hope will be of service to me in after life.

You must take good care of yourself and children. Do not whip them. I believe it is best to let them be unrestrained than to be punishing. All children are bad and unruly. Do not let Will study too hard. I was glad to hear he was head again, and hope he will remain there. I will bring them all a pretty present. How I do wish to see you and them, and yet we are separated a thousand miles by railroad, etc.! This is a long distance when I think of it. Tell Anna she must be a good girl and I like to hear that she cries when my letters are read. I hope to see Frank much grown when I return, and I hope also to see my dear wife recovered and in good health, with blooming cheeks again. I hope you are pretty well; but you must not get well too quick.

I hope the servants are doing well. If they do not, it is best to let them alone and not have any difficulty with them. In Washington they had white servants entirely. Here they have black ones. I get along with the black ones best.

I will write you from New York, if I have time. I hope to see some one from Greenville. General Thompson told me to write him when I returned, and he would go back with me.

Give my love to your mother and family and kiss the children for me.   Yours truly and affectionately,

B. F. PERRY.

NEW YORK, July 20th, 1846.

MY DEAR WIFE: I shall leave here in the morning for Albany, in company with Colonel Fair and Mr. Nance. We will go thence to Niagara Falls, through Lake Ontario, down the St. Lawrence to Montreal and Quebec, which we expect to perform in six or seven days. We shall then return through Lake Champlain and Lake George to the Hudson and Saratoga Springs. There Colonel Fair will leave us and return home. I shall call to see Mr. Van Buren and stop at West Point, then go to New Haven, Newport and Boston, and return by way of the Virginia Springs to Greenville about the middle of August. Mr. Nance will return with me. He is a very worthy and clever gentleman and I am much pleased with him as a traveling companion.

I have been in New York only two days, and would not leave with regret for the beautiful Hudson, had I received a letter from you whilst here, as I hoped and expected to do. I feel sure you have written and the letter has been misplaced in some way, which provokes me. You do not know how dear a letter from home is to one in a strange city. My heart sank within me when the bar keeper informed me that there was nothing for me in the postoffice. I made him send again, and again the same answer was returned. I console myself with the hope that you and our dear little children are all well. I do not think I shall ever wish to leave home again to travel. I am not sorry, however, that I am making this tour. It was discreditable to me never to have been to the North, but I shall be satisfied when I return to my home, to my wife and children.

I wrote you from Philadelphia, which letter I suppose you have received. We had a pleasant trip to New York, passing through a beautiful country, the heart of New Jersey, in a high state of improvement, adorned with many pretty little villages and towns—Princeton, Newark, Burlington, Jersey City, Elizabethtown, Amboy, etc. I stopped at the Astor House and find it a most magnificent hotel, well kept. I rather think the best table I ever was at, but the company is inferior. At table we have soup, which is one course, then fish; then all sorts of meats and vegetables, oyster pies, etc.; then all sorts of pastry, strawberry pies, puddings, etc., etc. Then the cloths are removed and we have pineapples and all sorts of fruits; and lastly, ice creams. If I can get one, I will send you a bill of fare. The servants are all white, and very attentive. I now see so few negroes that when I see one I feel as if I had found an acquaintance, and feel glad to see him. I feel as if *he* was my countryman and fellow-creature and not the white man. To-day we wished a carriage to drive to the Croton water works, and I selected a black man instead of one of the many white men standing by. I think Cuffee was made for a servant, and he does pretty well at his post. In every room of this hotel there is a Bible placed on the table.

I called to see Hastie to-day. He was out. I left Nichols' letter and my card. The weather has been quite cold, but to-day has been very pleasant. I rode through the Park, saw the Museum and there met two mammoth boys, seven and ten years old, weighing five hundred pounds. They look like fat hogs. As I return I shall endeavor to see more of this great democratic and mobocratic city. The streets are crowded from morning till 12 o'clock at night; so much so that it is difficult to walk them. I went to Trinity church Sunday evening, but the pews and aisles were all full. I stood up amid the crowd till the organ stopped and then went out. It is the largest and richest church in America, I expect.

You must write me to Boston, as soon as you receive this letter. I shall be constantly traveling now for a week, and you may not hear from me in that time. Accept my love for you and the children and remember me to your mother and family. I must now pack up. Your husband.

B. F. Perry.

Albany, July 22d, 1846.

My Dear Wife: I cannot resist the temptation which a few leisure moments afford me of writing to you. I have nothing to write, and yet it gives me pleasure to say so, and to know you will take a pleasure in receiving such a communication from your husband in a far distant land. I wish I could only receive a similar communication from my wife to-night; but that pleasure will be denied me until my return to New York and visit to Boston.

I wrote you on leaving New York. I will now bring my journey up to this time:

Tuesday morning we got on board the steamboat for Albany. From the time we started until we reached this city, the scenery on the Hudson was a continued picture. To me it was an enchanted view the whole way. I did not know before that a landscape could be so beautiful. It is worth travelling a thousand miles to see. The beautiful rivers, the high and precipitous banks, rugged cliffs, splendid mansions, lovely farms, fertile and highly cultivated and improved, the flocks of cattle, etc., all drew from me admiration and wonder. The boat was crowded with men, women and children, several hundred. I took my seat in the extreme part of the forward deck and continued to gaze on the bewildering scenery. Colonel Fair and Mr. Nance joined me, and Mr. Hobby, Assistant Postmaster General, united himself to us. He was familiar with every spot and could point out every house, and cliff and village. He was born on the banks of the Hudson. I found him a most intelligent and agreeable gentleman, very much like Mr. Calhoun in appearance, and talks like him. I never saw a prettier place than Newburgh, a town on the Hudson. The Catskill mountains looked to me very much like the Saluda mountains.

We reached this city at 5 o'clock. The British Legation, Mr. Cranston, was on board—a very plain looking gentleman. Albany is a beautiful town, built on the side of a hill and on top of the hill. Every rain washes the paved streets clean. The convention of New York is now in session at this place. We went last evening to visit the Capitol and were very politely shown over the House by one of the members. Mr. Townsend. In the morning I found that Mr. Cambreling and Mr. Kemble were members of the convention and boarding at the house we stopped at. I sent them Mr. Poinsett's letters and they were very civil to me. Mr. Kemble is one of the most accomplished gentlemen I have met with, a bachelor, and as I was told in Washington, the "Siamese friend" of Mr. Poinsett. I have had a great deal of conversation with him. Governor Wright is not at home to-day. My letter to him I will keep till I return. Mr. Cambreling is a very plain, sensible gentleman, but not remarkable for anything except, perhaps, his good sense.

We start in the morning for Niagara Falls. It is now raining very hard and I am afraid it may rain to-morrow. The next letter I write you will be from Her Majesty's dominions, and in it you may expect a description of Niagara and the lakes.

Tell Will I will bring him a nice suit of clothes from Canada. Tell Anna and Frank I will bring them something pretty, and I must get a present for you from Queen Victoria's realms.

My dear wife, good-night. All of my letters are written in great haste, as I have not time to travel, look, write and sleep all at the same time. It seems to me I have been in one continued hurry from the time I started. Travelling is not pleasant, except that you see so much.

Remember me to your mother, Susan, McBee and Anne. Good-night.   Affectionately your husband,

                                        B. F. PERRY.

SARATOGA SPRINGS, July 23d, 1846.

MY DEAR WIFE: I arrived here last night, very much fatigued and worn down. Enclosed I send you a letter which you will read and send over to Colonel Townes. It will give you some idea of where I have been, and I have not time to re-write it for you. I shall leave here this evening for Troy, Albany, Van Buren, Springfield, New Haven, Boston, etc. I shall not get your letters until my return to New York. It seems to me that I have been almost to the end of the world, and am happy that my face is now homeward. You may well imagine my impatience to return to my wife and children. I am heartily tired of travelling and will never care to go from home again.

In Montreal I purchased three beautiful dresses for you: one of silk, one of a new sort of goods, which has not yet reached the United States, and the other a most lovely pattern—silk and woollen. I have purchased Anna two beautiful dresses, perhaps enough for three or four. I have purchased Will and Frank a suit each. I have also purchased for you a great many Indian curiosities, which are beautiful, bags, pin cushions, etc. And also a variety from the Grey Nuns. I have bought for myself some fine clothes, all very cheap. Your dresses are new and lovely.

How glad I would be to hear from you, but I flatter myself that you are now perfectly well and that the children are all well. It has been more than a month since your confinement, and I hope the bloom is restored to your cheeks. This is the very first opportunity I have had to write you since my letter from Albany.

Last night I met here some very pleasant ladies from South Carolina, who seemed glad to see me because I was from their own State: a Miss Nelson, from Statesburgh, who knows the Bradley's and says one of them is to be married to Richard Harrison in a short time. She is a young girl about eighteen, and I have walked with her all over the grounds, to the Springs, etc. Miss Yates is here and has taken possession of Colonel Fair. There is a Miss Taylor here from South Carolina, granddaughter of Governor Taylor, and a pleasant girl. Mr. Seabrook and his bride, Miss Bulow, are here, who seem pleasant and glad to see us. There are at this house about five hundred persons; some thousands at the other houses. The world seems congregated here.

In some of my former letters I spoke of the heat breaking out over my body. The skin is now all peeling off and my

hands look bad, but are now pretty well peeled over. I shall
have a new fresh skin on my return. Yesterday I was bilious.
I feel much better to-day.

I shall part company with Colonel Fair and Nance at Troy,
and I regret it, but they will not wait on me. I must see Governor Wright and Mr. Van Buren before I return. When I
shall reach home I do not exactly know. I wish to spend a
day or two in Boston and a day at New Haven. I may stop
a day in Washington and a day at the Virginia Springs.

God bless you, my dear wife and children. Kiss the children
for me, and give my love to your mother and family and remember me to all my friends in Greenville. I shall have a
great deal to tell you on my return—enough to keep us talking for a long time.   Your affectionate husband,
                                        B. F. PERRY.

NOTE.—His letters, describing Niagara Falls, Montreal, Quebec and the Lakes, were
written to the Mountaineer, and he did not repeat to me

KINDERHOOK, August 3d, 1846.

MY DEAR WIFE: Enclosed I send you a letter to read and
hand to Colonel Townes. I have nothing to add to it. I wrote
it because I had a few leisure moments.

I was very much gratified with my visit to Mr. Van Buren,
and spent the evening most pleasantly. When you see Mr.
and Mrs. Poinsett, say to them that Mr. Van Buren, Mr. Gil-
pin and lady, Mr. John Van Buren and Mrs. Van Buren all
desire to be remembered to them, and spoke of them in the
most affectionate terms; said they were in hopes to have seen
them here this summer.

By waiting to see Mr. Van Buren I have lost two days, and
I assure you I hesitated whether to do so or not. I thought,
however, that you would desire it, and that you would be
willing to postpone the pleasure of seeing your husband that
length of time for him to make the acquaintance of the ex-
President. I was pleased with Governor Wright, too, but had
a few moments to stay only before the cars left.

Colonel Fair and Mr. Nance have gone. They are to meet

me at New Haven to-morrow night. They will be returning from Boston and I shall be going on. My impatience to return home is now so great that I shall not enjoy what I see as I otherwise might. I will write you from New Haven, if I have time.

I must now close my letter and start for the railroad. God bless you and the dear little children, and God only knows how much I wish to see you all again.   Yours truly,
                                        B. F. PERRY.

NEW HAVEN, August 4th, 1846.

MY DEAR WIFE: I arrived in this lovely town yesterday evening, in time to take a walk around the college buildings, the State House and churches. This morning I procured a large open barouche, and drove all through the streets and around the suburbs. Oh, my dear wife, how happy I should have been to have had you seated by my side, pointing out the streets and houses as you saw and recognized them. The house in which your mother lived, the church which you attended, the school where you went every morning with books and slate, like a sweet little girl of ten or twelve—sometimes trudging through the snow and meeting the cold winds I need not say to you that New Haven is dear to me from these associations, and if it were an ugly place, still I should love it, as the town in which my dear wife was educated and spent some of her most pleasant days. But it is the prettiest town I have yet seen. I was told by a young Englishman with whom I travelled in Canada, that New Haven was the prettiest town in America. I now heartily agree with him. But it is twice as large as when your mother resided here, and yet every house is built in the finest style and with great taste.

After I had ridden over the town, I drove to Colonel Moseley's to deliver your mother's letter. He was not at home, and would not return for several days. So I shall not have the pleasure of seeing your old friend. I left the letters and my card and drove to Governor Edwards'. He was at home, and as soon as he broke open your mother's letter, came into the room. I found him very pleasant and agreeable. He made a great many inquiries about your mother and her family. After a short call I took my leave and returned to the Assembly House, where I have stopped. I had hardly returned before he came round and told me that on reading your mother's letter she desired him to introduce me to Professor Silliman and President Day, and show me your sister's grave. He stopped at Mr. Ingersoll's to inquire the spot. We went into the cemetery and readily found the place beside the grave of a daughter of Commodore Shubrick, in Mr. Ralph J. Ingersoll's inclosure, and shaded by a small tree planted some years since. I need not say to you that I shed many tears over the grave of my wife's sister, as I looked on it. My weakness was seen and noticed by Governor Edwards.

We found Professor Silliman at home, and I was much pleased with him, his conversation and his appearance. He is really a fine looking gentleman and much younger than I expected to see him. He begged to be remembered to your mother and to you; said he remembered all of you with great interest and thanked me for calling to see him, and regretted my stay was so short. We found President Day engaged with the Board of Trustees. He came to the door of the college and expressed great pleasure at seeing the son-in-law of Mrs. McCall, inquired most affectionately after you and your mother and invited me to take tea with him this evening at half-past six. He said Mrs. Day would be glad to see me and inquire about Mrs. McCall. Governor Edwards asked me to walk round this evening and see his daughter, the only member of his family living with him, but I am afraid I shall not be able to do so. We rode by the brick house in which your mother lived, near the college. I looked at it with great interest, and pictured to myself three little girls, blooming with health, beauty and loveliness, playing and running over the house and garden, and that one of them was now my wife and the mother of three sweet, lovely children! What a change a few years makes in the condition of a little girl!

I can not get from here to New London except by riding twelve hours in the stage. I will return to Springfield and from there to Boston. I will pass through either New London

or Newport on my return to New York. Say to Mrs. Butler I came hereon purpose to go by Mrs. Rodgers' to Boston,
but am disappointed. I hope, however, to have the pleasure
of seeing some of her relatives on my return.

I hope to hear from you in Boston and also on my return
to New York. I must close. Shall not write you again for
some days. Kiss the children and give my love to your
mother and family and remember me to all my friends.

      Yours truly and affectionately,   B. F. Perry.

             Boston, August 6th, 1846.

My Dear Wife: I arrived here yesterday to dinner, and
received two letters from you. I can not tell you how happy
those letters made me. It had been so long since I had heard
from you, and I had travelled so many thousand miles, that
it really seemed to me I was lost and forgotten. I was afraid,
too, that some of you might not be well. If I had consulted
my feelings, I should have started home from New Haven,
without visiting Boston. But I am now better satisfied, and
will remain here a day or two. Your first letter was advertized and I did not receive it till I applied for advertized letters.

I immediately, on reading your first letter, made a memor-
anda of the articles you wish me to purchase and which I will
get as long as my money holds out. I purchased last evening
a beautiful shawl, such as you described, white, with lilac
stripes, for $3.50; the price was $4. It is a beautiful thing,
and far prettier than anything of the kind ever sold in Greenville. Your dresses in Canada were about $9 apiece. The dres-
ses for you and the children were $35. My cloth clothes—dress
coat, and pantaloons and travelling sack—were $52. My
clothes in Washington and shirts in New York $60. Carriage
hire has been a large item. I paid one day in New Haven
$3.25 for the hire of a carriage to ride over the city and to
visit with Governor Edwards. I mention these things to show
you the state of my finances, and if I should fail to bring you
a music box and something else, you must know it is not because I would willingly deny the least request you can make.

It has been my great pleasure since our married life commenced to love you and make you happy in everything.

Colonel Fair and Mr. Nance have gone home. They did not pass through New Haven, and I saw nothing more of them. I found on my arrival at the Tremont House a letter from Col. Fair explaining why he did not meet me as he promised. Just as I was getting into the cars I met Mr. Latta, of South Carolina, going to Boston, and will make the same stay that I do and return to New York with me. He is an old gentleman of great wealth and has a son and two daughters at school in New Haven. He was on board the vessel with your father and mother when they were going to Philadelphia, where your father died. He desired to be remembered to your mother, about whom he made many inquiries. I find him a pleasant old gentleman, and being from South Carolina, we have attached ourselves to each other.

The weather is extremely hot, and last night I was so much fatigued that I had a dreadful headache. I was afraid I was going to have a bilious attack, and hunted for Dr. Crook's pills, but they are lost. This morning I feel much better, but the weather is so hot there is no moving about.

Tell Mrs. Butler that I will certainly see her sister, but I will not be able to visit Newport. I will return through New London to New York, there stay a day and go home as fast I can. I should like to call and see your uncle, Captain McCall, but am afraid I shall not be able to do so.

Tell Susan that the coral beads must be a present from me and not you. I claim the honor of making the young stranger the present.

Tell Will, Anna and Frank that their commands shall all be obeyed, and that they must be good children, mind what you say and not be cross to each other.

Yours truly and affectionately,   B. F. PERRY.

BOSTON, August 7th, 1846.

MY DEAR WIFE: Enclosed I send you a letter for Colonel Townes. I shall leave in the morning for New London and do not know when I shall have time to write you again.

I have purchased for you a most magnificent bracelet —$11.50, and two gold pins $3. I have had made for you the prettiest thing in the shape of a French cap your eyes ever beheld—$5. How I shall carry it without mashing is the difficulty. I have purchased a beautiful set of coral for Susan's first-born—$4.50. I have purchased a suit of clothes for Will and Frank, at $17. They are very handsomely made. I will make your mother a present of Massilon's Sermons, which I now have. My trunk is full and I can get nothing more in it. You see I have gratified your every wish. I felt it doubly my duty to do so, as I had been off enjoying my travels and spending money while you were at home. I wish you had been with me, and yet I know you would not have found it pleasant.

I must now pack up and be ready to start soon in the morning. Good night, my dear Liz. Kiss the children for me.

Your affectionate husband,
B. F. Perry.

Richmond, August 12th, 1846.

My Dear Wife: I am happy to be this far on my return home to you and the children, and I am very much tempted to go on by Charleston. Judge Butler and many others are going that way. But I do not consider it entirely safe, and if I returned through Columbia I should have to stay there at the Court of Appeals.

The morning I left Boston I received your last letter, and on my return to New York I found two more only. The two first you wrote me are lost in some way. I was delighted to receive all your letters and read them over the second time in the cars as I came on.

When you see Mrs. Butler tell her I was much pleased with Mrs. Rodgers and her family. If Miss Rodgers' wardrobe had been completed, she would have come on with me. Her mother says she is insane on the subject of her visit to South Carolina. She will remain twelve months with Mrs. Butler and will come on in September. She is about the age and size of Behethlind Butler, and seems quite a pleasant girl. I was very much

pleased with Mrs. Rodgers, who must have been a very handsome woman when young. Her sons seem remarkably clever.
One is in the navy and the other in the army and goes to
Mexico in September. There was a little chap about thir-
teen or fourteen, who was standing with a string of crabs
in his hand, looking at me. His brother called him and said
to him: "You have let that gentleman see you with your
crabs, and he is a relation of ours." "Well," said the little
fellow, "I saw him when he got out of the boat, and I thought
then he was some of our kin."

I have just had a visit from James' mother and brother. She
is quite a good looking woman, about the color of James, and
seems smart and sensible. James must take his bad qualities
from his father, who ran away to a free State, as his mother
tells me. She gave me a letter, a brooch and twenty-five cents
to give James. The brother of James looks lazy, too.

I did not see General Thompson on my return to Washington. He will leave there in four or five days with General Butler,
by the way of the Virginia Springs.

Miss Rodgers informed me that Miss Thompson and Mr.
Jones were engaged, and Miss Crayton and Mr. Rowland.

Governor Butler looks to be in very bad health, a mere wreck
of himself. His difficulty with Mason is unsettled and I did
not hear the particulars.

I must now conclude, as I have to pack up and eat breakfast in time for the cars. I hope to be at home in the course
of ten days, or perhaps sooner. I do not know the stage route,
etc., and cannot speak with certainty.

Kiss the children for me and remember me to your mother
and family and all friends.   Your loving husband,
                                          B. F. PERRY.

ANDERSON C. H., Oct. 28th, 1846.

MY DEAR WIFE: I have time only to write you a few lines
by Butler Thompson, who starts this morning. He told me
that his mother said I must come back by Thursday. I suppose from that you will be invited to the wedding. If so, I
hope you will go. I trust Frank is better and that neither of

the other children has taken the scarlet fever. If you can, write
me by Thursday's mail, though I do not know whether I shall
be detained here so long.

We have very little business in court, and as soon as I can
get through I wish to go to Pendleton and perhaps see Mr.
Calhoun's farm, etc., thence to my mother's old place. You
must write me to Pickens by some one who is going.

*　*　*　*　*　*　*　*　*

My dear Liz, our happiness in this life is very much in our
own hands. If we strive in the right way to be happy, we will
be. We must exercise Christian philosophy and bear up with
the ills of this life, look to the comforts we have and not pine
after those we can not get. My rule through life has been to
make the most of my situation and look on the bright side
of the picture; never worry myself about that which cannot
be altered or has passed by, do my duty to the best of my
ability and care little as to consequences; and I flatter myself
that I have been blessed through life; blessed with prosperity,
blessed with the comforts of life and the good opinion of my
acquaintances; blessed with a good wife and pretty children,
to whom I look for all my future happiness, and to promote
whose happiness I live and am happy.

Your affectionate husband,
B. F. Perry.

ANDERSON, October 29, 1846.

My Dear Wife: Mr. Speer will return to Greenville in the
morning and I cannot forego the opportunity of writing you
a few lines.

I hope to hear from you and how the children are by the
stage to-morrow. I have been detained here longer than I expected, and the probability is that I shall not get off till the
end of the week. I have a case of great importance which is
at the foot of the docket. I have been trying to compromise
it, but have not yet succeeded.

I had a settlement with my client Mattison, and took his
note for $200. He is very good, but I should like to have the

money, instead of it. I shall get another note for $50, so the profession is not entirely valueless.

I have not yet sent your pin-cushion and box to Mrs. Sharpe, but will do so, if I do not carry it myself. I have not seen Mr. Sharpe since I have been here

General Whitner told me to-day that Mrs. Whitner had sent to invite me there yesterday evening, but the messenger could not find me, and she was scolding him for not bringing me. They are kind and hospitable.

I hope you and your household are doing well. I am very anxious about the children, but hope for the best. You must write me a letter by Mr. Speer to Pickens. Send it to Mrs. Rowland's early Sunday morning and let me hear all the news; how you and the children are, how your mother and family are, the servants, etc. You can also give me an account of Eliza Thompson's wedding. I understand the whole world is invited.

I am very much afraid I shall not be able to go by my father's old place. I am certain that I shall not get there Friday night, but perhaps I can see them at Pickens and it will do as well.

We shall have a great deal of business at Pickens and I may not be at home till the last of the week or Sunday.

The railroad is quite popular here and in Abbeville. It is said Abbeville will subscribe $500,000. I begin to think the road must go that way.

Kiss the children and tell Frank I will let him ride Skylark When I come home. Tell Will he must keep head, and tell Anna she must be a good girl and begin to learn her letters.

Your affectionate husband, B. F. PERRY.

PENDLETON VILLAGE, Friday Night.

MY DEAR WIFE: I am this far on my way to Josiah's. After waiting all the week, I discovered this evening that my case would not be reached in time to try it.

I received your letter yesterday morning and was very glad to hear you were all well, except Frank, and that he would be in a short time. I am under constant apprehension that Willie or Anna will take the scarlet fever. You must be sure and write me at Pickens court.

I did not get here till dark, and since tea I have sent your box to Mrs. Sharp. The messenger has not returned yet. I shall not be able to call and see her in the morning, as I wish to make an early start. I hope, however, to see the Greenville stage before I leave, and read the Mountaineer.

I suppose Miss Eliza Thompson was married last night and feels quite happy in the change she has made. How happy all persons ought to be immediately after marriage. They have all the pleasures of married life in enjoyment and expectancy, without any of the cares and responsibilities. I shall expect an account of the wedding in your letter at Pickens court.

By the by, I have been reading Mrs. Ellis' book on " Women, Daughters, Wives and Mothers." It is a capital work and I must purchase it to read to you this winter, on my return from Columbia. She gives some most excellent advice.

You say the North American Review came with a criticism on Simms' works. I wish I had it to read whilst here at Pickens. I will write a letter to-night to John Cunningham. I am glad you wrote Miss Pamela. I have no doubt she is sorely grieved at Simms' unkind attack on her. John's letter was a sensible one.

I am here at Hubbard's hotel. The fare is as good as ever. They have just moved back from Georgia.

You must take good care of the children. I hope your mother is better. When I was there and saw everything in the house looking so handsome and so neat, the table spread with a fine breakfast, the situation so beautiful, I thought to myself, where should happiness dwell, if not here? In passing along the roadside I very often see some miserable hovel, dirty and squalid children, no carpets, nothing pleasant to see, and yet, I think to myself, it may be the inmates are happier than some others with all the comforts and luxuries of life!

But good-night. Happiness should be and has been our companion so far, and our abode is a fit habitation for it, and we are worthy of her companionship. Good-night.

Your devoted husband,   B. F. Perry.

PICKENS, November 3d, 1846.

MY DEAR WIFE: I have only time to write you a line by Colonel Townes, thanking you for your letter by Mr. Elford. I was indeed glad to hear you were all well and doing well. I do not know when I shall return, perhaps not before the last of the week. I was disappointed in going to Josiah's, as it rained all day, Saturday, and I was detained at old Pendleton. I have not yet seen Josiah or Foster. They will be here to-day.

In the evening of Saturday Mr. Sharpe called to see me and thanked me for the pin-cushion and invited me to his house, but I did not go. Sharpe was dressed up and looked quite spruce; had a good deal to say about his farm, etc.

I came to this place Sunday morning and escaped the rain, but have a bad cold. I find very little business here. General Thompson says he is going to quit riding the circuit. Says if he practices law he will go to Charleston.

In great haste. You must remember me to the children and kiss them.   Your affectionate husband,

B. F. PERRY.

TO HIS WIFE IN CHARLESTON.

COLUMBIA, S. C., Thursday, November 24th, 1846.

MY DEAR WIFE: Your letter was received last night. I was glad to hear from you. I am gratified to know you are pleasantly situated at your aunt's, Mrs. Turnbull's, but you did not mention anything about the children. Always tell me how they are and what they are doing.

I would have written to you last evening, but had not an opportunity of doing so before the mail closed. I wrote a very good letter for the Mountaineer, as you requested, and gave an account of our railroad meeting in Charleston, etc.

We met with a considerable accident on Sunday coming to Columbia. There were three cars filled with members of the Legislature. I happened to be in the front one. The car behind ran off and broke the axle-tree, pulled off the middle one and twisted the one in front considerably. Finally the hindmost car broke loose and was left behind. The engine was stopped and the second car, after great difficulty, was extricated from the train. Fortunately no one was hurt. All the members had to get into one car and stand up till they reached Columbia, a distance of thirty miles. The other two cars were badly broken and left behind. It was late at night when we arrived in Columbia. The cause of the accident was the weakness of the hindermost car.

I found all of our Greenville members in Columbia, and at Gladden's. They brought no news from Greenville. Colonel Townes said he had seen Edward and Charles. Colonel T. P. Butler is here, but returns home to muster his company. He says he will go to Mexico if his company accepts the terms. which I am inclined to think they will not. Major E. D. Earle is here in good spirits and so is Reed. The candidates for the different offices are without number: thirty-two for messenger, ten or fifteen for Secretary of State and as many for Superintendent of Public Works.

I saw Mr. W. Gilmore Simms and had a long talk with him about his criticism of Miss Pamela's book. He has written an answer to John Cunningham, which I presume will pacify. He said he had no idea that the article was written by a lady.

Mr. Boyce came to me on Monday, and said that some of the Senators had been trying to get Colonel Patterson not to run for President of the Senate again, and if he had consented they intended to elect me, but that Patterson seemed so anxious about it, they did not like to say more to him on the subject. How would you like to have heard of my election as President of the Senate, without in fact my knowledge of what was going on? I have been asked repeatedly, since my arrival here, if I had no aspirations to the Chancery Bench.

The prospects of our railroad is brightening. Colonel Memminger called to see me yesterday and we were engaged some time in consultation on the subject. He takes a deep interest in it. We have another meeting this evening.

B. C. Yancey has his bride with him at Hunt's. I am going over this evening to see her. Ben looks well, but I saw a tear in his eye when I spoke of his marriage. Perhaps it was in remembrance of his first wife. It seems disrespectful to the departed wife. To take another seems like being divorced or forsaking the memory of her.

Kiss the children for me and give my respects to all your aunt's relations.   Your affectionate husband,

B. F. PERRY.

COLUMBIA, November 26, 1846.

MY DEAR WIFE: Your second letter was received last night and gave me great pleasure to hear from you, but I was surprised you had not heard from me. My letter was certainly in the postoffice when you wrote. You must not wait for me to write you an answer. This you know I would do most cheerfully, if I had time; but really, between the Legislature, the courts and calls of company, I have not a moment to spare. I have been wishing to go to the theatre and to see the painting again, but have not time. The night you declined the Miss Elliots' invitation I had to walk a half mile down to the college in the night and back, after 10 o'clock. The wind was terribly cold. The Board of Trustees meet again Monday night.

You seem to think you will be short of money. You know, my dear Liz, I will send you more if you desire it. Make yourself easy on that score, and if you see anything you desire, purchase it and write me and I will send you the money. It gives me great pleasure always to gratify the wishes of my wife in every particular. I know how pleasant it is to purchase little things which we fancy.

There is one thing which I wish you to do for me—and you must do it. As you pass through Columbia you must let Clark Mills take your bust. It will look handsome and be much better than a portrait. I have had mine taken. He came to my room, took a brush and put on my face a sort of paste which dried in a few minutes and fell off a complete mould for a likeness. The operation is not disagreeable. He says he will have the finest likeness of me he ever saw. I saw Mrs. David F. McCord's. It is very fine and looks well. The price is $25 and $35. You may have copies for $5 and $7.50. His busts of Judge Johnson and Elmore are admirable. Also of Pettigru, Preston, Judge Cheves, and Hampton.

I have paid McCarter $200 for my book bill; also paid over the money received of Butler Thompson. Whilst I was sitting for my bust, Dr. Teague came in and paid me $50 in part towards a counsel fee. I thought the visit very opportune.

General Thompson and the Greenville delegation think I can be elected Chancellor, but I do not. Colonel Ashe said he would vote for me in preference to any of the candidates. Colonel Fair has suggested me as president of the bank, in place of Elmore, who will be elected United States Senator, but I have suggested Judge O'Neall. If he is elected I do not know but that I may be a candidate for the Bench. I am really gratified at the estimation in which I seem to be held by the Legislature. Dr. Goodwin told me the other day that he was very anxious to see me President of the Senate. He is Senator from St. Matthews.

You must write me often and all about the children, yourself and aunts. Colonel Martin asked me this morning how often you wrote me. He said his wife wrote every other day and he did the same. You must write me when you expect to come up, or what your arrangements are, as soon as you determine.

I have not yet been to pay Mrs. Yancey a visit. We have a railroad meeting in Columbia to-morrow evening. We are all to make speeches. Colonel Summer will publish my speech in the Carolinian next week.

I have engaged with the editor of the Southern Review to write an article on "Curwen's Life," and embody the Revolutionary history of the upper country.

I must now go to the committee room. Tell Will he must be a good boy. His papa was never so bad (though I was a bad boy at his age.) Tell Anna she must be the young lady and Frank a little man. Kiss them. My love to your aunts.

B. F. PERRY.

COLUMBIA, S. C., November 29th, 1846.

MY DEAR WIFE: I was very much disappointed last night, on returning from the railroad meeting and not finding a letter from you. My first letter to you remains unanswered. I hope, however, that you and the children are all well and that I shall certainly hear from you this evening.

I am so busy that I have no leisure on Sunday, even. The whole of to-day I have spent in drawing a railroad charter for Greenville. Last night I made a speech an hour long on the railroad to a town meeting in this place. General Thompson is to speak Monday night. Then I have to meet the Board of Trustees and elect a professor of Roman literature.

Yesterday I attended a lecture of Dr. Ellett's before the trustees on gun cotton. I loaded a pistol with this cotton and shot it three or four times. The cotton is better than powder and will supersede it in all probability.

To-morrow my resolution giving the election of electors to the people comes up for discussion. We shall begin this week to have matters of interest before our honorable body. I wish you were here to witness them. You must let me know as soon as you determine what you are going to do, whether remain in Charleston or come to Columbia. General Thompson says Mrs. Thompson is to be here this week. Jones and Eliza have gone home from Edgefield.

Clark Mills is making progress with my bust. At present it is an ugly affair. I desire very much to have yours taken. I am sure it will make a handsome one; and whenever an opportunity offers I wish to have your portrait taken.

How I should like to see you and the children—peep in on you and see how you are employed. I hope the children are behaving well. But really no children *always* behave well, and should seldom be taken from home. I must now go to dinner, and will keep my letter open till night.

I have just received your letter, dated Saturday morning, and thank you for it. I was afraid you were unwell or something was the matter with the children. I have written you twice and hope you have received the second letter.

I shall be glad to see you whenever you feel disposed to come up, and will supply you with all the money you wish. I know how pleasant it is to spend when abroad, and how much we are tempted by pretty things. I only regret I have not a fortune to place at your command. But we have done pretty well. If you stand in need of funds, write me. Ask Klinck to give you a bill of the groceries.

I have just received a Greenville Mountaineer with my letter in it and one from Colonel Townes.

Mr. Elmore will not be a candidate for the Senate. Judge Butler will be a candidate, Colonel Davie, Barnwell Rhett, Pickens, Judge O'Neall, Governor Hammond, etc.

I must now conclude with my usual requests to the children and your aunts.   Affectionately,   B. F. PERRY.

COLUMBIA, December 2d, 1846.

MY DEAR WIFE: I received your letter to-night and herewith inclose you a check, which I hope you will receive safely and that it may be as much as you will need. I do not think you will save much by remaining in Charleston, as there are so many pretty things to tempt you. The next week is the gay and fashionable week in Columbia. The commencement in college is on Monday, the ball that evening. The inauguration of the Governor-elect will take place Wednesday. He will no doubt give a party. I went round to Dr. Roach's this evening to see General Thompson. He and Mrs. Thompson will stay there, also Mrs. Walker and Jane. Mrs. Roach told me that she could furnish me with a fine room the first of next week. You can stay there or at Clark's Hotel. He has room plenty, and I desire you to stay in Columbia a few days and see the town.

I went to the Fair to-night and saw an immense concourse of ladies and gentlemen. Colonel Hampton and his family were there, selling all sorts of pretty articles. There were twenty or thirty different establishments belonging to different persons. I bought a pen of Miss Yates for fifty cents, a beautiful thing; two jellies of Colonel Hampton's family for twenty cents. At another table Mr. Griffin bought a couple and paid $1. The difference in price, and in persons, too. The Fair was a most magnificent collection. Colonel Martin had bought some little matter to send in a letter.

Governor Aiken and lady paid us a vist this morning, in the Senate Chamber. He introduced me to her, and I took a seat

by her and conversed with her for some time. Their little
daughter was with them. How immensely rich she will be! I
saw Mrs. Ben Yancey at the Fair. She is immensely rich.

I hope you see the Charleston Courier, which contains an
account of our legislative proceedings. I made a speech on
the electoral question, Tuesday, about an hour long. Colonel
Dargan replies to me, and I shall reply to him.

You must write me as soon as you determine to come. If
you could come up on Sunday next you might be at the college
commencement. If on Tuesday you can be at the inauguration on Wednesday; but you can use your own convenience.
Take special care of the children on the railroad. Perhaps
one of your cousins may come up with you—Alston or Arthur Hayne. It would be well to have some friend to come
with you. If you desire it, you may stay until after the adjournment of the Legislature, and I will come down for you,
and then I know you will be safe under my charge; but be
careful, and do as you like best. It gives me great pleasure,
my dear wife, to gratify your every wish, when I can do so.
My happiness in life is to make others happy, and the greatest
to make my wife and children happy. I live for them.

Good-night. Kiss the children. If Will comes up I should
like to keep him until I go home. Remember me to your
aunts.   Your affectionate husband,
                                            B. F. PERRY.

P. S.: General Thompson and Col. Herndon had a fight yesterday, in Gladden's Hotel, but through Chancellor Johnson
and myself they have made friends. Col. Herndon said at the
supper table that the General was broke. Erwin Jones told
Thompson. He met Herndon, told him he lied and struck
him in the mouth, and thereupon a scuffle ensued. Duncan
ran for me, but it was over; neither hurt. They shook hands
to-day and made friends.

COLUMBIA, S. C., December 5th, 1846.
MY DEAR WIFE: I was very much disappointed to-night in
not receiving an answer to my letter inclosing you a check.
I hope it is not lost. I received a letter from you night before

last. I have been so much engaged that I have not had time to write you as often as I wished to do.

We have had more elections and electioneering than I ever knew before. After five ballotings, Judge Butler has been elected United States Senator. Governor Hammond ran ahead of him two ballotings. Colonel Davie was also a candidate. There was great excitement.

The election of Governor will be made Tuesday. Chancellor Johnson has already resigned. Two Judges are now to be elected. My friends here placed my name amongst the candidates for Chancellor, but I do not know that I will continue to run. They think, however, that my chance is a good one for being elected. I have no such thought Gen. Caldwell, Mr. Mr. DeSaussure, F. Wardlaw, Colonel Patterson and Haynsworth are all candidates. For the Law Judge, General Whitner and Colonel Dawkins are running. But for Whitner I would run for a seat on the Bench. A great many persons have spoken to me about running and have persuaded me that my chance was as good as any one's. But the other's have had so long the start of me.

You had better not come here until the elections are over. They will probably take place next week; but you must expect to hear of my being beaten, and as all my friends say, it will do no harm to run, if I am beaten. I believe, too, it is your advice. My Union principles prevent my success in gaining office. It is well I do not care for honors.

I was at the Fair last night and saw Jane Walker. Mrs. Walker is here and her son. I wrote you in my last that Mrs. Thompson, Eliza and Jones were here.

I hope you have seen the Charleston Courier and read the account of my speeches. I am sure you will read them with great pleasure.

I saw Mrs. Aiken in the Senate Chamber to-day and conversed with her some time. She has been there every day for the last three or four days. I find her a very pleasant lady. Mrs. Yancey was in the Senate Chamber to-day, but I did not have an opportunity of speaking to her. I met her last night, at the Fair again.

I was invited to dine at Mr. DeSaussure's to-day, and also

with Colonel Martin, but I declined both invitations.

How are the children. You must write me several days be-forehand, when you are coming, so that I may prepare to re-ceive you; but you had better not come here during the elec-tion, if I run for Chancellor. I will write you again Monday.

In haste, yours truly and affectionately,

B. F. PERRY.

P. S.: I bought of Miss Hampton, at the Fair, a silk waist-coat worked by her; also a pretty workbox for you—the prettiest thing you ever saw.

COLUMBIA, December 7th, 1846.

MY DEAR WIFE: I have just received a note from Colonel Martin, informing me that Mrs. Rhett has this afternoon lost a little daughter with scarlet fever, and that it is prevailing in several families in Columbia. I feel great apprehensions about the children when you come to Columbia. If the fever continues, you must either remain in Charleston or pass im-mediately through Columbia. I will write you again to-morrow evening, and you must write to me what you deter-mine on.

The election of Chancellor takes place to-morrow, at 1 o'clock. The probability is no election will be made the first or second balloting. I shall be voted for by some, but have no thought of being elected. Caldwell and DeSaussure are elec-tioneering hard for it. I think it unbecoming a gentleman to electioneer for such an office, and will not even mention it to a member. It is not generally known that my name is used as a candidate. Several gentlemen have told me that they were glad my name was used, although they could not vote for me on the first ballot, they would the second. My friends tell me that all the members seem pleased at my nomination, and that the greater portion would support me but for the pledge to others previously. In the scramble there is no tel-ling what may happen. The fact of my permitting my name to be used will do me no harm, if I gain nothing by it. I look upon it as an honor to be taken up, under the circumstances, and voted for by even a few friends; but I will write you the result to-morrow night. The election for Law Judge will not come on for several days.

I was at at the commencement this morning, and a splendid one it was. More company and better performance than I ever witnessed before. Mrs. Jones was there, also Mrs. Walker and Jane.

In regard to servants, clothes, etc., do as you think best. I have confidence in your judgment and. prudence, my dear wife. My only anxiety now is about the children. I have so many reports to write that I must conclude.

Your affectionate husband,   B. F. Perry.

Columbia, S. C., December 5th, 1846.

My Dear Wife: * * * * * * Now for the election I would not go to the State House at all this morning. I never mentioned to any one that some of my friends were going to vote for me. Dr. Goodwyn, who sits with me, did not know it. The members were all pledged to vote for others, but all expressed themselves friendly towards myself. Caldwell received 36, Wardlaw 30, DeSaussure 27, Patterson 25, Haynsworth 19, myself 12, Dargan 6, Young 2, etc. There is no election made. I presume Caldwell will be elected.

I care nothing about it. In fact, I had rather stay at the Bar. But General Thompson and others persuaded me that it would be no injury to me to have public attention drawn to me as a candidate. But I was not a candidate. My friends, only, voted for me—a few of them.

I will expect you Saturday evening. I hope there is no danger of scarlet fever. The cars arrive now before night, and leave Charleston at 9 o'clock in the morning. I will be most happy to meet you and the children, my dear wife. After all, the only real pleasure in life is one's own family.

I saw Mr. Legare this evening, who spoke of you. Mr. Bull introduced him to me. I saw Dr. Hayne, also, this evening. General Thompson and Mrs Walker will leave before you arrive. I will endeavor to get a room at this hotel for you.

My bust is said to be a fine likeness. The man who cut my likeness on paper several years since is here now. He is cutting the whole Legislature. You and all the children may have your likeness cut.

There was a great to do here to-day. The volunteers arrived here from Chester and paraded through the district. They will be in Charleston to-morrow.

I am now engaged in court constantly. I am glad to hear you are pleased with Charleston and your friends there.

You must write me again before you come up. Let me hear from you Friday night.

I must now conclude. Kiss the children for me. I am very anxious to see the little creatures. I hope Anna and all of them have improved by their visit to the city. Tell Will I shall expect to see him a man in behavior.

Yours truly and affectionately,
B. F. PERRY.

COLUMBIA, December, 9th, 1846.

MY DEAR WIFE: I received your letter to-night, and shall be prepared to greet you at the railroad depot Saturday evening. I do not suppose there will be any danger of the children catching scarlet fever. It will give me great pleasure to meet you all again. It seems a long time since I saw you, and I have been in a hurry ever since; not time to do anything.

I made a speech of one hour's length to-day, in the Senate, on the railroad, which drew a great crowd and was well received. To-morrow I speak on the electoral question, which is made the special order at 1 o'clock. To-day I have been in court a good deal. I wish you were here, to be present when I speak.

The election of Law Judge will take place to-morrow. Colonel Dawkins, Whitner, and Withers are candidates. Who will be elected I know not. General Caldwell was elected Chancellor.

I have just returned from the Board of Trustees. We have elected two professors—Pelham and Williams.

I must prepare for my speech in the morning, and therefore must conclude.

Colonel Townes is unwell. I heard from Greenville. They are all well there. Colonel Hoke wrote me that my negroes were doing pretty well. Jim and Minerva had had a fuss and he came very near sending both of them to jail. I received a letter from Mr. McBee about the railroad.

I shall expect to see you with great anxiety and pleasure, on Saturday evening. You must not disappoint me. Take care of the children.

Give my love to your aunts. Thank your aunt, Mrs. Turnbull, in my name, for her hospitality and kindness to you and the children. Your affectionate husband,

B. F. Perry.

Columbia, Wednesday Evening,
December, 16, 1846, 6 o'clock.

My Dear Wife: I hope by this hour you are comfortably seated in our home, with the children all around you, eating their supper, and the servants coming in to see you. To-day we have had rain, and I have thought of you all the time; but you were fortunate to escape so well. I hope you had a pleasant trip and that the children gave you no annoyance.

Yesterday I dined with Colonel Martin, who invited the President of the Senate, Colonel DeTreville, Moses, Boozer, etc. I like Martin very much. He said the first thing he thought of when he saw the sun rising Tuesday morning, was that you would have a pleasant day to travel.

Dr. Goodwyn told me that Mrs. Goodwyn was coming to our room to bid you good-bye, but found we had gone to bed. She had taken tea out that evening. Colonel Davie spoke of my pretty mountain children, whom he had seen running about in the piazza.

The likeness of the whole family, by Brown, is finished and makes a pretty group, as Colonel Ashe says. I have got a gilt frame for it. You look quite natural. Your dress and hair are taken very accurately, and I think your features also. Mine is not so well as the others. Anna and Frank show rather better than Will, but all look well enough. Will is standing near me and Anna near you; Frank between.

I have to go down to the Senate to-night, at 7 o'clock, and will finish my letter when I return. Colonel Townes, Sam Earle and Edward H. Earle, all go up in the morning. I will send this letter by Colonel Townes.

It is now 11 o'clock in the night and I have just returned from the State House through a terrible rain and deep mud. This is one of the worst nights I ever saw. How glad I am you are not travelling. We have had a great deal of discussion to-night in the Senate and I feel much exhausted. I claim the credit of having saved many thousand dollars for the State this night.

I have just heard of a most melancholly death. Mrs. Seabrook, once Miss Bulow, the wife of a member of the Legislature, married last summer and I met them at Saratoga Springs, gay and joyous. He was a very young man and his wife not more than seventeen years old. She died suddenly. Her husband went to the railroad to-night and heard of her death. He fainted and appeared for some time a maniac. Another member, Mr. Barnes, of Lancaster, lost his wife last week in the same way.

I must now bid you good-night. I hope to meet you Sunday evening. Kiss the children, and give my love to your mother and family.

The subscription of the State to the railroad has failed.

Yours truly and devotedly,
B. F. PERRY.

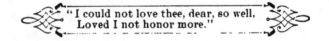

"I could not love thee, dear, so well,
Loved I not honor more."

LETTERS

Received Acknowledging Receipt of Second Series of "Reminiscences of Public Men," by Benjamin Franklin Perry, and Considered by His Wife Worthy of Preservation for His Descendants.

GREENVILLE, S. C., Sept. 2, 1889.

Mrs. B. F. Perry:

DEAR MADAM: Words are scarcely adequate to convey to you the gratitude I feel for the many favors received from you in the presentation of the several volumes containing Reminiscences and Sketches by ex-Governor B. F. Perry—Tributes and Letters commemorating his memory, and Addresses delivered by him on so many important occasions.

His fame will increase while the history of South Carolina survives. Not until the events of the late struggle between the North and the South are forgotten will his name cease to be remembered. As the fame of the country increases, so will *his* fame expand. He will ever stand forth in the history of the State as one of the grandest characters South Carolina has ever produced, and held up as a model for the young men of the country in future generations to imitate.

His position while Governor of South Carolina in 1865, was one of the grandest spectacles any country ever witnessed. He was at the time the only one the down-trodden people of South Carolina looked to for deliverance from their almost helpless condition. He was the grand mediator between the conqueror and the conquered, and maintained the confidence and respect of both sides in the efforts for reconstruction. What a grand spectacle he presented to the world! Oh! how much the South owes to Governor Perry! In vain talk of his grand achievements being erased from the page of history! He stands at this time, and will ever loom up in the minds of unborn generations as one of the greatest patriots that this State or country has produced.

Oh! how much the country is indebted to you for your noble efforts in perpetuating his fame! You will ever stand in history as one of the greatest wives the country has ever known. England and the civilized world honors and will ever love and cherish the devotion of Queen Victoria for the memory of her husband. Such will ever be the esteem in which you will be held. Your name will ever be cherished while the songs of devotion are heard.

But I must conclude, knowing that my zeal and respect for the memory and virtues of my departed friend may carry me too far. Please accept my humble thanks for your great kindness. May you live many years to enjoy the fruits of sincere affection which you have so faithfully exemplified. God bless you and yours.   Most respectfully your friend,

ROBERT McKAY.

COLUMBIA RECTORY, 13th Sept., '89·

My Dear Mrs. Perry:

Mr. Leaphart left the volume, second series, of Governor Perry's writings at the Rectory for me, with the request that I would acknowledge its reception to you.

You are bringing hundreds of your fellow-citizens under obligations to you, my dear Mrs. Perry, for these volumes. They contain so much of our history that is unwritten, and so many of Governor Perry's admirable addresses to the youth of our State, and withal, so rich a collection of biographical matter, that they make a most valuable addition to my library, and will make a rich and lasting monument to your departed husband's wisdom, patriotism and exalted worth.

I have just finished reading, with intense interest, his History of Nullification and of the Conventions of '32 and '33·

It must be, indeed, a labor of love to you to arrange and publish the writings of your husband, now that God has taken him from you! It is like communing with him in person, and I know you find it a great comfort, for I know well how you loved him, and how devoted he was to you.

What a solace to our sorrows and disappointments it is to realize that those who die in the Lord are infinitely more blessed in their rest and peace in Paradise than they were here, in the changes and chances of our mortal life!

And this is your solace, in your great bereavement; for never have I seen a child fall asleep more humbly and more trustfully on its mother's breast, than did Governor Perry give himself up to his God and Saviour, when the summons came to him at Sans Souci!

Live in the constant presence and faith of Him whose grace and love are alone sufficient for us, dear Mrs. Perry, and it will not be long before you are united to the society of your husband, your dear old mother and Hayne, Frank and Anna and all the loved and lost!

This is our faith, revealed to us in the Gospel of our salvation, and kept and taught by the Church of Christ. May its consolation abound to you.   Most truly your friend,

ELLISON CAPERS.

COLUMBIA RECTORY, 15 Sept., '89·

My Dear Mrs. Perry:

Reading the account of the Provisional Government in South Carolina, I missed the *State papers,* to which Governor Perry refers. They would add so much historical *interest and value* to the account, if published. I wish you could have published them in this volume. Then the Governor's history of his work, so patriotically and nobly done for his State and his people, would have been complete. I noted in reading *twelve* of these papers, which must be on file in Washington, if you have not copies of them. I will mention them in order, as they are referred to by Governor Perry:

Page 247—His Proclamation: This does him great honor and is a most important State paper. The newpapers of the time all have it, but you know such publications are too soon lost and forgotten.

Page 255—Communication showing the status of our people as to taking the *Test Oath.*

Page 270—Official letters to the President and Secretary defending his order respecting the Provost Marshals.

Page 271—Important Proclamation respecting courts, etc.

Page 273—Letters to President Johnson.

Page 275—Message to the Convention: A most important historical State paper.

Page 279—Message to the Legislature: Equally important.

Page 282—Letters to the President; also another message to the Legislature.

Page 284—Letters to the President and Secretary.

Page 287—Long letter to the Secretary of State.

Page 289—Appeal to the President in behalf of certain petitioners.

Page 290—Letter to the Secretary of State, touching the direct tax, etc.

All these papers illustrate the period, the people and your noble and faithful husband. Pity they could not have gone in this volume, to the exclusion. if necessary, of some of the less important Sketches. If I had known your plan for this book, I would have made the suggestion to you sooner.

But the book, *as it is*, is most valuable, and the truest and most enduring tribute your devoted love could pay the memory of your faithful husband. Most sincerely yours,

E. CAPERS.

UNITED STATES CIVIL SERVICE COMMISSION,
WASHINGTON, D. C., Oct. 11, 1889.

My Dear Mrs. Perry:

I have just received your letter of the 10th inst. I will gladly do my best to comply with your request, but I doubt whether I shall be able to get copies of the papers which you want. I am sure that it will not be possible to obtain the originals. I think it probable that copies of the papers from the Senate cannot be obtained without special order of that body, which of course cannot be obtained until Congress meets. To get copies of the other papers it will be necessary to have the consent of the President and of the members of the Cabinet. I have never met the President except officially, and I know no member of the Cabinet except Mr. Windom, the Secretary of the Treasury. In the discharge of my official duties I have no occasion to meet the members of the Cabinet. You will understand, of course, that I have no right to ask for copies of the papers, and that if given to me it would be as a personal favor. There is a rule in some of the departments, and perhaps in all of them, that copies of papers on file shall not be given except to members of Congress or to persons who can show in writing that they are entitled to them. I mention these facts to show you that it will not be possible for me to obtain the copies as promptly as you desire, and that perhaps I shall not be able to get them at all.

As a Democrat, I cannot expect favors to be accorded to me at the departments, and my official position does not entitle me to consideration as a matter of right.

I will do my best to comply with your request, but you will see from what I have said that it is by no means certain that I shall succeed. If your son would write to the President and to each of the Cabinet officers, asking for copies of the papers, I believe that he could get them. As the son of Governor Perry, and as a member of Congress, he has a right to copies, if any one has, and I am sure that his request would receive consideration.

I make this suggestion as the speediest and surest way of accomplishing your purpose, and not because I am unwilling to do what you ask. I have no doubt that the order for copies of the papers on the Senate file can easily be obtained when Congress meets.

Another advantage in his making the application is the fact that copies, if furnished to him, would be without cost; whereas, if made for me they might, and probably would, put you to needless expense. I trust that you will consider this suggestion, but if for any reason you prefer not to act on it, I will do my utmost to get the copies for you.

Permit me, dear madam, to assure you that it will always give me sincere pleasure to serve you, and to express my regret that it is not in my power, by virtue of my office, to call for what you want from the Executive Department.

Yours very truly and respectfully,
HUGH S. THOMPSON.

MRS. B. F. PERRY, Greenville, S. C.

P. S.: The suggestion as to Colonel Perry's asking officially for the papers was made by a gentleman familiar with the workings of the Departments, who called at my office after I began to write, and whom I consulted as to the best means to carry out your wishes. I am sure that his suggestion, if adopted by you, will enable you to accomplish your purpose, if it can be done at all. H. S. T.

NOTE.—It will be seen by the preceding letter that I am following the advice of our beloved friend and pastor, Rev. Ellison Capers, and endeavoring to obtain the official papers he alludes to in his letter; and if successful, I will have them published, with an account of the Provisional Government, in a pamphlet entitled: "State Papers Connected with the Provisional Government of South Carolina in 1865."

MRS. B. F. PERRY.

UNITED STATES CIVIL SERVICE COMMISSION,
WASHINGTON, D. C., Oct. 21, 1889.

Dear Mrs. Perry:

I called at the White House last week and left there a written memorandum of the papers which you want. You will see from the enclosed letter, which I have just received, that none of the papers are on file there. When your son comes to Washington I will confer with him about the matter, and perhaps we shall be able to find the papers, if they are on file in the Department of State.

From inquiries made in another quarter, I am inclined to believe that President Johnson did not leave on file in the Department of State or elsewhere in Washington such papers as you describe. Yours very truly and respectfully,

HUGH S. THOMPSON.

EXECUTIVE MANSION,
WASHINGTON, Oct. 19th, 1889.

Hon. Hugh S. Thompson, Washington, D. C.:

SIR: I find that there are no papers whatever of President Johnson's administration on our files here, he having taken away with him everything of the sort. It is barely possible that there may be some official communications of Hon. B.

F. Perry at the State Department, in which case I should think Mrs. Perry could obtain copies through her son, Congressman Perry.   Very truly yours,
                                E. F. TIBBOTT,
                                    Executive Clerk.

                        CHESTER, S. C., 10th Sept., 1889.
Mrs. B. F. Perry:
  MY DEAR MADAM: There came to me by mail last week another volume of speeches, sketches, etc., from your distinguished and venerated husband, and I am thereby placed under renewed and increased obligations to you.
  My estimate of the life and character of Governor Perry grows upon me continually, as the day of his departure recedes further and further into the past. The image of the flesh and blood in which his noble soul inhered, perhaps has faded somewhat from my mental vision, but his magnificent and instructive life and character grows broader and brighter upon me day by day. The people of the State owe it to themselves to give a tangible and patent expression of the high regard in which I know they hold his memory by erecting, at the door of the new Federal Court House in Greenville, his full length statue in lasting marble. It would give me pleasure to contribute to such a worthy cause. With kindest regards I am,
                                Yours truly,
                                GILES J. PATTERSON.

                        BIRMINGHAM, ALA., Aug. 20, 1889.
Mrs. B. F. Perry, Greenville, So. Ca.:
  MY DEAR MADAM: Yesterday morning your very kind and most acceptable letter reached me, and about dusk the three books came. The type of womanhood which is South Carolinian could alone have conceived and executed your kindness. I lay it to my heart as my chief honor that I was born

of the mother that was mine, and that she was a South Carolinian.

My brother-in-law sat on one side of the lamp and I on another far beyond our usual hour of retiring, reading the fascinating books. I believe, indeed, it was near daylight ere we surrendered to Morpheus. He being a Virginian, found all things new. I luxuriated in the pastures long familiar to me. There was old Mr. David Gregg, so familiar to my boyish memory, with "faith" and "work," making corn! When I was a child taking riding lessons behind my father on the horse, he would stop us on the way. "Good morning, Colonel," to my father. "Well, Mr. DuBose, how is your health this morning, sir?" to me. Judge Evans, whose son married my aunt; General Williams, whose son married my aunt; Chancellor Dargan, whose brother married my aunt, and he himself my cousin; Governor Miller's two wives were my cousins; Governor McDuffie, as I learned after I was born, used to visit my father and get my mother to sing to the piano, that he might fall asleep after he went to bed (the ball in his back kept him awake); Colonel William Wallace, whose brother, Dr. John Wallace, married my aunt—All of these and many more came up life-iike to me, and played athwart my fancy in delightful pranks. You are from Charleston and I read of Judge Frost. His son Thomas married my cousin and very dear friend.

The books, my dear madam, are *real* books. I shall read them carefully. Already I see somewhat of the light that shone on the path of the remarkable man, their author. When I may claim the time—within a month I hope—I will write to you fully my contemplations. The beautiful memorial you have erected in their pages to your beloved husband, stands a testimony to the capacity of your sex for the most elevated and most spotless consecration of spirit.

With reiterated thanks for the generous emotions your kindness has aroused in my own bosom, I beg to subscribe myself,

Most respectfully your friend and obedient servant,

JOHN WITHERSPOON DuBOSE.

BIRMINGHAM, ALA., Aug. 25, 1889.

Mrs. B. F. Perry, Sans Souci:

MY DEAR MADAM: You have probably received my acknowledgment of the receipt of the books and my thanks for your favor to me in sending them. I have studied them with unfeigned delight.

When I was a lad I received my first impressions of Governor Perry. My youthful imagination was excited in admiration of Mr. William R. Tabor, Jr., the young and brilliant editor of the Charleston Mercury, for the Mercury came to my father's house ceaselessly even before my birth. Mr. Tabor delivered an address to the fifth year's meeting of the class of which he was a student in the South Carolina College, and the subject was "Public School Education." Mr. Perry criticized the address in his Greenville paper. Mr. Tabor challenged Mr. Perry to the field of honor. I had never received any lessons of adverse opinion to the *Code*, but in this case I was involuntarily impressed with the haste of Mr. Tabor and with the correctness of Mr. Perry's position and with the calmness of his reply to Mr. Tabor, declining his challenge. I think Mr. Perry acted wisely.

I am greatly pleased to be able to review, in the columns you have published, the sentiments and motives of a Union man. Of all Union men Governor Perry was most consistent, and his untiring participancy in politics needed only the record you have made of his acts and opinions to erect of his earlier career a landmark which will endure, to indicate most important facts of history not otherwise available. His Union principles were peculiar and therefore inestimable in the firmness and intelligence and sagacity with which they were advocated. Mr. Yancey sought to perpetuate States' Rights and to prevent the revolutionary assault upon slavery threatened by the North. Mr. Perry was as much devoted to these purposes and general results as was Mr. Yancey. The explanation of the difference between the methods proposed by the two leaders, constitute the value to the world of the writings of Governor Perry. In this light the whole range of American history, from the May Day, 1765, on which Patrick Henry astounded the great men of Virginia by his resolutions against the stamp act, to this instant is thrown wide open to the most profound inquiry, by the columns you have sent forth showing your husband's analysis of great principles and his conclusions reached in earnest investigation. It will be impossible for future historians to avoid Governor Perry's writings and saying this, I pay to him the highest honor my words can convey.

Nearly one-fourth of the national life of Americans has been spent in war, not estimating Indian wars in the West. Governor Perry's theory of politics inculcates reliance upon the agency of *peace* to accomplish the ends of national honor. Certainly a pioneer in that theory may contemplate the *failure* of war to accomplish the *objects* of war with *great self-satisfaction*.

I do not mean to be understood as intimating culpability of the South in the late war. The South proposed no breach of the compact of the State and the sections. Governor Perry points out the facts of adverse Northern construction of Southern rights. He differed from the majority of the South in the matter of remedy only, and in this light, as I have said, his views become of historic interest, *invaluable and everlasting*.

The literary style of the entire work is a welcome relief from the false imitations of classic authors, now in vogue, and from the vulgarity of superlatives, hyperbole and misrepresentations common to most of the alleged "Northern histories" with which the times are afflicted.

The scorn of tyranny and the unmeasured contempt of military usurpation which these books instill into the public mind are so forcibly put that they cannot be read without purifying the public life. They will take rank along with Plutarch.

With highest esteem I beg to remain, dear madam,
Your friend and most obedient servant,
JOHN WITHERSPOON DUBOSE.

SPARTANBURG, Aug. 19th, '89·

MY DEAR FRIEND: Yesterday's mail brought me the second series of Governor Perry's Reminiscences. I waited to read some of its pages before writing you.

I find the reminiscences of great interest, the sketches of prominent men, especially those of our own State, are graphic and most valuable as photographs of the history they helped to make.

The Provisional Government is a page of unwritten history that you have crystalized. I do not believe that you yourself realize how good a work you have wrought in giving to the public these volumes. The perfect honesty with which the narratives are illumined, the lucidity of style, the fine humor displayed, make the sketches so life-like that when history is written these pages will be continually a mine of reference. I need not say that I thank you warmly for the book you have sent to me. * * * * * * Your affectionate friend,

CELINA E. MEANS.

SPARTANBURG, Sept. 19, '89·

MY DEAR FRIEND: I must write again and tell you how much I have enjoyed your last brought out volume. Several persons, amongst them Dr. Carlisle, have said to me that this is of greater interest than any of the others. I think that you have showed fine discrimination in its selections. The parts of history are of real value now, and in twenty years will be invaluable. * * * * * * * * * *

It seems a long time since we've had a letter from you, so do try, if you have time, and write very soon. Love to Fanny and Emily and for yourself. Very lovingly,

CELINA E. MEANS.

SUMTER, S. C., Aug. 28th, 1889.

Dear Mrs. Perry:

It was with pleasure that I received "Second Series of Reminiscences with Speeches and Addresses" by ex-Governor Perry, sent me through your kind remembrance.

In my college days it was always a pleasure to me to read anything emanating from the pen of your revered husband; and
now, in the maturity of middle life, I know of no author
whose writings I peruse with a greater degree of satisfaction.

We can all, and more especially the youth of our land, be
benefited by a study of the works of his master mind.

I remember well, in the genial atmosphere of your ante-
bellum home, how much we looked up to and respected Major
Perry. His dignified and manly bearing impressed all with
whom he came in contact. I remember his conscientious regard
for duty; I remember his love for his native State, and his
mighty efforts to stop the tide of popular fanaticism that bore
us on to a long and bloody war; I call to mind when the die was
cast and South Carolina had declared herself once again a free
and independent State, his language: "South Carolina is going to ruin, and we will go there with her." And from that
time on, the Palmetto State and our own sunny South had no
truer, stronger or more faithful subject than your honored
husband.

Would we had more of such men in this day and time, to
pilot the South through the devious paths of uncertainty
that beset her, upon whose strong arm we could lean, as upon
one whose eye and mind could not only discern the signs of
the times, but look beyond and see the political future towards
which we should set our course. But God willed that he should
go up higher. "The world is better that he lived," a beautiful
epitaph; we feel it within our souls, and cheered by his noble
example would so conduct ourselves that this might as truly
be said of us when we pass hence. Thanking you for the privilege and pleasure of reading this work—given to the world
by the devoted wife of him whose memory every South Carolinian loves to honor and revere, I remain as ever,

Very truly your friend,
JOHN S. HUGHSON.

FORT MEADE, FLA., Aug. 30th, '89.

DEAR COUSIN: I cannot express my appreciation of your
kind favor, the latest publication of Reminiscences with

Speeches and Addresses, by your distinguished husband. I
have had time to-day to read a little and look through it.
Think I shall like it more than any preceding ones. Dear
cousin, had not this noble work of love been left to engage
your mind and heart, you surely would have died with him.
Your love for and admiration of him is *grand*. When I read
those tender lines to-day on the first page, dedicating to his
posterity the eloquent and beautiful thoughts of his great
mind, and in conclusion giving expression, in the most pa-
thetic, impassioned words to the deep, pure, eternal love, that
death itself cannot change, tears of sympathy rolled down
my cheeks, and you felt nearer and dearer than ever before.
With all your ambition and pride, you loved as only woman
can. Your devotion reminds me of Josephine to Napoleon,
but your object was more worthy, and with him life was
sweet and worth living, and to him you could ever say: "My
love shall be a crown of glory to thy brow, and not a feeble
hindrance in thy path."

I am so grateful for your kind remembrance of me. I hope
your health is good. Love from us all to you and cousin
Fanny.   Affectionately your cousin,
                                         LUCY F. PERRY.

GEORGETOWN, S. C., Aug. 30, 1889.
Mrs. B. F. Perry, Sans Souci, Greenville, S. C.:

DEAR MADAM: I beg to acknowledge the receipt of a copy
Second Series of "Reminiscences, with Speeches and Addresses," by your distinguished husband, and to express my
sincere appreciation of your courtesy in placing at my command a volume whose contents are an imperishable monument to the purity, ability and public spirit of one of South
Carolina's most noble sons. Time is said to be a great solvent
and leveler: It is also a wonderful vindicator, as the career
of Governor Perry strikingly demonstrates. Nothing could
more completely illustrate the inextinguishable vitality of
truth and the power of devotion to duty to live down obloquy
and conquer hate, than the spectacle of a statesman whose

life was at one time embittered by suspicion and saddened by
mistrust, dying at last with the love and admiration of his
fellow-citizens, shedding a halo around his couch and soothing
his last moments with their gentle benediction.

When I think of Governor Perry and his Cato-like firmness
of soul, I am reminded of Horace's picture of the man "*inte-
ger vitæ scelerisque purus,*" and find a new significance in the
words "*mens sibi conscia recti.*"

The book which your allegiance to his memory has inspired
you to publish is a valuable contribution to the history of
South Carolina politics, as well as a charming addition to her
literary treasures. It ought to be placed in every public and
private library in the State, and should be read by every
youth whose proud privilege it is to call himself a South Carolinian.

Pardon the liberty which I—a stranger to you personally
—have taken in thus writing to you at length, but I feel con-
strained to express my gratitude to you for placing on record
so complete a picture of one whose name will always add a
lustre to the fame of his native State.

Yours very respectfully,
WALTER HAZARD.

ATLANTA, Sept. 17th, 1889.

MY DEAR MADAM: Accept my sincere thanks for the Second
Series of Reminiscences with Speeches and Addresses, by your
distinguished husband. This work will always hold its place
among the most valued in my library. I shall read it with
great pleasure and with pride in the thought that I am a native of Governor Perry's State.

While he represented sentiments different from those held by
my family, I have always admired his eminent ability, sterling
integrity and fearless independence of character. Living he
honored his State, and dying left an added lustre to the name
of Carolina.

With the highest regards I remain, my dear madam,

Your obedient servant,
PAT CALHOUN.

Mrs. B. F. Perry, Sans Souci, Greenville, S. C.

CLARK's HILL, S. C., 30th Sept., 1889.

Mrs. B. F. Perry, Greenville, S. C.:

DEAR MADAM: Prolonged absence has prevented an earlier acknowledgment of your thoughtful kindness in sending me a copy of the "Second Series" of your distinguished husband's "Reminiscences."

I have read the beautifully bound volume with absorbing interest and valuable instruction.

Governor Perry's mind was so comprehensive, his perceptions so accurate, his analysis so correct, his memory so tenacious, his sense of justice so high and his independence so fearless, that his recorded impressions of the remarkable persons and events of his time will be more and more prized each year in the future. His "History of Nullification in South Carolina" will henceforth rank as the standard authority on that momemtous subject.

Although he lived in the most exciting and trying period of the State's history and was ever opposed to the prominent theories of her polity, yet his honesty of purpose and integrity of character were never questioned by any one, and the sagacity of his foresight as well as the soundness of his judgment in politics *must now be conceded by all.*

Again thanking you, I remain, Very truly,

G. D. TILLMAN.

STATE SUPERINTENDENT OF EDUCATION,⎫
COLUMBIA, Oct. 9th, 1889. ⎭

DEAR MRS. PERRY: Your volumes grow in interest. This last of the second series are invaluable to any one who wants to know about the men who helped to make our State famous. The Reminiscences are a string of pearls and the friends of the distinguished dead will place great value upon them. I note only one—the brilliant orator and gifted scholar, W. K. Easley, the most accomplished gentleman on his circuit. Then the history of the various State Conventions and the Provisional Governorship should go into every library.

The Governor did a great work, and you equal it by preserving and perpetuating his labors.

With warmest thanks and kindest remembrances to your household, I am, Very truly and respectfully,

JAMES H. RICE.

GEORGETOWN, S. C., Oct. 10, 1889.

Mrs. Governor B. F. Perry, Sans Souci, Greenville Co., S. C.:

MY DEAR MADAM: I have received the three volumes which you were good enough to send me for the library of the Winyah Indigo Society, of this place, and thank you sincerely and gratefully for the same. I deem it very fortunate that this honored old society, itself a monument of the generous nobility of South Carolinians, shall have upon the shelves of its library the record of the life and deeds of so noble a gentleman and citizen of the State, for the perusal, study and emulation of our children in the future.

Your devotion to the memory of your worthy husband is itself one of those refreshing things which must cheer every true man to deserve the love and affection of his wife and to lead a life worthy of commemoration.

With sincere prayer for your happiness, I beg to subscribe myself. Yours with esteem,

R. DOZIER,
Pres't W. I. S.

AIKEN, S. C., October 15th, 1889.

Mrs. B. F. Perry, Greenville, S. C.:

DEAR MADAM: I received on yesterday, by express, a copy of the "Reminiscences, with Speeches and Addresses, by B. F. Perry, ex-Governor of South Carolina," second series. I thank you for it.

History is, in great part the record of the struggles and achievements of the illustrious dead. When a true and impartial history of South Carolina shall be written, the name of Benjamin Franklin Perry will adorn one of its brightest pages, and his fame and glory will be upon the lips of men while integrity and statesmanship are honored in our land.

Permit me, as one of the many who revere your husband's name, and take a lively interest in your welfare, to express the hope that your declining years may pass in unalloyed contentment, cheered and comforted by a people's love, and when the summons shall be served, come up higher! may it be the lot of he who cherished you in life, to welcome you in his present home, a home among the immortals.

With the kindest wishes, I have the honor to be,

Very respectfully yours.

JAMES ALDRICH.

WILMINGTON, DEL., Oct. 18, 1889.

DEAR MADAM: Permit me to acknowledge with thanks the volume of Reminiscences by your husband, the late Governor B. F. Perry, of South Carolina. I shall read them with much interest, and am much indebted to you for the opportunity.

THOMAS F. BAYARD.

Mrs. B. F. Perry.

(From Hon. Hugh McCulloch, Secretary of the Treasury in the Administrations of Presidents Lincoln, Johnson and Arthur.)

WASHINGTON, LOCK BOX 646, Oct. 21st, 1889.

DEAR MADAM: I have had merely time to glance at the volume of Sketches which you were so good as to send to me with your letter of the 15th inst., but I have seen enough to satisfy me that you have been the skillful compiler of very interesting and valuable articles.

The books which you have sent to me are not only valuable in themselves, but they will be of great service to the Southern historian of the Civil War.

Governor Perry was a *very wise and far-seeing* statesman, and if his advice had been followed the terrible and most destructive of wars would have been avoided.

I wish I could be sure that great race troubles were not in store for South Carolina. I can only express the hope that they will not come in your day.

Very truly and respectfully,

Mrs. B. F. Perry. HUGH McCULLOCH.

GEORGETOWN, S. C., Oct. 25, 1889.

Mrs. B. F. Perry, Sans Souci, Greenville, S. C.:

MY DEAR MADAM: Please accept my very sincere thanks for a copy of First Series of Reminiscences by the late Governor B. F. Perry, of this State, which you have had the kindness through me to send to the Winyah Indigo Society, of this town. It will afford me great pleasure to place it upon the shelves of the Society's library, where it will be read with delight and profit, not only by our present citizens to whom the Governor was well known, but by those who shall come to fill our places long after we shall have passed over the "River," and to whom Governor Perry will be only a shining character of history. Allow me, my dear Mrs. Perry, to thank you in advance for the other books which you have so kindly and graciously promised to send me as soon as they shall be published. Everything emanating from Governor Perry or relating to his conduct during his long, useful and honorable life, will be cherished by Carolinians as illustrating the services of one of those rare prototypes of manly beauty, intellectual power, and moral courage, which were so eminently embodied in the person and character of this distinguished counsellor of the State and friend of man.

With renewed thanks for your kindly attention, I am,

With great esteem,

R. DOZIER,

Pres't W. I. S.

UNITED STATES CIVIL SERVICE COMMISSION,⎰
WASHINGTON, D. C., Oct. 31st, '89·⎱

Mrs. Governor Perry :

MY DEAR MADAM: I was called home by the birth of a son. On my return to Washington I find your more than courteous letter and the three interesting volumes, which I shall read with the most careful attention. I have enjoyed the first volume greatly. I hold in high esteem many, very many, of South Carolina's statesmen, but none so high as those of the little group to which your husband belonged. It has always been my hope that some day I might write a history of movements in our country's life to which no historian, Northern or Southern, has yet done justice; and if ever that day comes, all four volumes you have sent me will be invaluable; and I trust I shall be able to do at least some feeble justice to the memories of the men of whom your husband was typical—the men who, more than any others, in any section, are entitled to the respect and admiration of those who, like myself, feel profound pride in all parts of our great Union.

Thanking you heartily for your courtesy, I am madam, with great respect, Very sincerely yours,

THEODORE ROOSEVELT

SHERBORN, MASS., Oct. 12, 1889.

MY DEAR, DEAR FRIEND AND COUSIN: I will commence this letter with a quotation from cousin Carrie Perry's letter to me: "Mrs. B. F. Perry, our dear cousin, sent me by mail the beautiful book she has (unaided) herself compiled from her dear husband's writings. I consider it to be a great honor to be thus remembered by so noble and interesting a woman as Mrs. Perry, and the book itself is a feast of knowledge and of noble thoughts and purposes, throughout a long and useful life; fascinating as the richest novel. It will be to me one of my treasures, and makes me long to see them again more than ever."

I can fully endorse the above, except "fascinating as the richest novel," as I never was fascinated with any novel—never in early life had any taste for them—but the writings of Governor Perry, and those of gifted minds and pure principles, will hold me entranced for hours, so that I would be insensible to scenes around me. (Even in early life I was thus entertained.) * * * * * * * * * * * * *

Love to all the dear ones. With love and gratitude,

Your afectionate cousin and friend,

CATHERINE HAVEN PERRY.

GREENVILLE, S. C., September, 1889.

MY DEAR FRIEND: Your highly valued present of Reminiscences of Public Men, with Speeches and Addresses, by ex-Governor Benjamin Franklin Perry, Second Series, is acknowledged with thanks, and is appreciated the more for the language of friendship to me personally, which you have kindly inscribed on a front leaf of the book.

The terse eulogies of your late distinguished husband, expressed in the numerous letters you have received from men of eminence, and other admirers of B. F. Perry, adds great value to the book in my estimation, and must do so with all his friends. I heartily congratulate you on having received so many such letters, and you have acted wisely in printing them. The evidence of the renown of ex-Governor Perry throughout this country, which these letters show, together with his own acts, writings, addresses and speeches, constitute a monument to his talents and patriotism more desirable, more expressive and more durable than one of marble. Long may you, the wife of B. F. Perry, live to enjoy the satisfaction afforded by the numerous tributes to his memory so fragrant with praises and admiration. Seldom has a lady found so many real sympathizers in her love and veneration of a noble husband as yourself.

With great respect,   Truly your friend,
                                          GEORGE F. TOWNES.

GREENVILLE, Nov. 13, 1889.
My Dear Mrs. Perry:

The enclosed acknowledgment of your very highly esteemed present was written soon after the reception of the book. It was laid aside and I have neglected to send it till now.

As time passes I am more and more impressed with the loss I have personally sustained by the death of Governor Perry. I find no successor to him in the pleasure his friendship and companionship afforded me. We always discussed together the current news—political, literary or social—and I greatly enjoyed his conversation. He was so communicative in regard to what he thought on all subjects, that I had the full advantage of his learning and insight in the deeds of men our cotemporaries as well as of the preceding times. He was an encyclopedia of biographical and historical knowledge. This is partially illustrated by his Reminiscences, but the living man was superior to his books. The reverse is often the case. Not a few great authors, like Goldsmith, have failed to impress their friends by their personal intercourse with any admiration of their genius and intellectual character. Not so with my departed friend, Governor Perry.

Yours with sincere regard,
GEORGE F. TOWNES.

HAMPTON, C. H., So. CA., 23d November, 1889.
Mrs. B. F. Perry, Greenville, S. C.:

MY DEAR MADAM: It is with most sincere pleasure that I write to acknowledge the receipt of the Second Series of Reminiscences of Public Men, with Speeches and Addresses, by your distinguished and lamented husband, the late Governor Benjamin F. Perry, whose name is so thoroughly iden-tified, and whose history is so closely interwoven with that of the State he loved so well.

It is a duty we owe to such men, that we preserve for pos-terity the record of their good deeds and the result of their lifelong labors.

I remember well the first time I saw Governor Perry. It was at the Democratic National Convention held in Charles-ton, in 1860. His magnificent courage and the splendid pic-ture he presented when he took the platform to vindicate his course in remaining in that convention when the majority of the delegates from the State had decided to withdraw, will never be effaced from my memory. The admiration which I conceived for him on that occasion was increased and inten-sified when, in after years, I knew him and learned to appre-ciate all the excellent traits of his character. Thoroughly posted in all the fundamental principles which underlie our government, devoted to the carrying out of those principles in their integrity and purity, and with a courage which never allowed him to falter where duty showed the way; his life will fill one of the brightest and most glowing pages in the history of his country and his State.

Allow me to thank you for the volume sent me and to wish

you God speed in the loving work of preserving for future generations the history of a great and a good man. I am, with great respect, Yours most truly,

JAMES W. MOORE.

LANDERS, FLOYD CO., GA., Nov. 25, 1889.

My Dear Mrs. Perry, Greenville, S. C.:

I received recently a package—being two volumes of your husband's speeches, literary and political, and a volume—memorial and letters of condolence to you.

Thanks for your valuable gifts and kind remembrance of one who made your acquaintance about fifty years ago. Though our paths in life have been in different States, I have cherished the memory of your gentle and lovable character.

As a youth I formed the acquaintance of your distinguished husband. I met him but a few times after my manhood, but I kept informed of his public career. Though I differed with him as to secession, I admired his moral courage and undeviating adherence to his convictions. With nearly his whole State against him, he stood unflinching to his principles. It was a very rare exhibition of moral courage. It stamped him as a noble specimen of a man.

As Provisional Governor, when in power, he took no revenge upon life-long, stern opponents; but, in kindness, wherever in his power, kept them and placed them in position. This fact testifies to the nobility of his character. From being one of the most unpopular men, he became one of the most popular in the State. The Legislature, not one of scalawags and negroes, but one controlled by the gentlemen of South Carolina—unanimously elected him a United States Senator. Honor to that Legislature, and a merited honor to your distinguished husband.

Again accept my high appreciation of your gift.

Your contribution to the memory of your distinguished husband presents a noble model to be studied and followed by our young men.

May Heaven grant to you a long life in the enjoyment of health and happiness. I remain,

Very truly your friend,

BENJAMIN C. YANCEY.

UNITED STATES SENATE,
WASHINGTON, D. C., Nov. 10, 1889.

My Dear Mrs. Perry:

I must thank you most cordially for the volume, Second Series of Reminiscences, with Speeches and Addresses, of your late husband, who was so distinguished in his day and generation, for his exalted character, eminent abilities and valuable public services.

I recur to my acquaintance with him and to the friendship he always honored me with with more satisfaction than any man of his day. The relations of cordiality that existed for so many years between our respective families is also a source of much pride and gratification to me. I value the volume very highly as an interesting contribution to history, and also because it comes from you. Allow me again to thank you.

Very sincerely and respectfully,

M. C. BUTLER.

Mrs. B. F. Perry, Greenville, S. C.

COLUMBIA, S. C., Nov. 26th, 1889.

My Dear Mrs. Perry:

Your very kind and highly appreciated letter was received last week. It would have given Mrs. Patton and myself the most sincere pleasure to meet you in our home on the College Campus, during your recent visit to Columbia, and we hope that you will find it convenient to call at some future time.

I am truly glad to learn that you are now engaged in writing the life of your distinguished husband. As a public man he is known and honored throughout the State and country; but he will now be "revealed" to us in his "domestic character," as you so happily express it in the letter which I had the honor to receive. One of the most interesting and instructive books in the annals of literature is "Boswell's Life of John.

son." In this biography he is portrayed not only as the poet and philosopher, but as the *husband*, and *friend* and *philanthropist*.

The numerous admirers of Governor Perry will be delighted to see him as he appeared to his own family and intimate associates in the retirement of *Sans Souci*. In his private as well as public character, as husband and father no less than as orator and statesman, he is, no doubt, worthy of our admiration and love. As I have said in a former letter, such a character will be a model which the young men of this grand old Commonwealth may safely imitate.

> "Lives of great men all remind us,
> We can make our lives sublime ;
> And departing leave behind us
> · Footprints on the sands of time."

You do me too much honor, my dear madam, in assuring me that the labor of love was undertaken in compliance with my suggestion. I took the liberty to suggest the preparation of such a volume at your hands, from a conviction that no other person was so competent as yourself to write his biography; and especially so well qualified to "reveal him in his domestic character," as was the companion of his life.

I shall be under additional obligations to you for a copy of the memoirs, as soon as published.

Mrs. Patton unites with me in expressions of the most sincere regard.   From yours, very respectfully,

E. L. PATTON.

NEW ORLEANS, Nov. 7, 1889.

DEAR MADAM: Many thanks for the two books containing speeches, sketches and reminiscences of your distinguished husband.

My intercourse with him during the war enabled me to form a correct idea of his noble character, and his conduct after the war, which only added to the lustre of his fame and enhanced the esteem in which he was held by his countrymen. When his opinions were overbourne in the councils of the

State, he bowed to the will of the majority, but with characteristic disinterestedness and charity, he did all in his power to ameliorate the condition of those who had neglected his warning voice.

You may indeed be proud of such a husband, and describe him as "the wisest, bravest, most unselfish statesman South Carolina ever produced."

With sincere regards, I am dear madam,

Yours most respectfully,

THOMAS J. SEMMES.

OFFICE OF CONGAREE IRON WORKS, ⎫
JOHN ALEXANDER, Proprietor, ⎬
COLUMBIA, S. C., Oct. 3d, 1889. ⎭

Mrs. B. F. Perry, Greenville, S. C.:

DEAR MADAM : The honor you confer upon me in presenting me through Mr. Leaphart, with a volume of Second Series of Reminiscences of Public Men, etc., by ex-Governor B. F. Perry, your venerated husband, is deeply felt and gratefully acknowledged. But this token is not needed to keep in ever-blooming remembrance the worth of the great deceased. His worth I had the fortune to know of while he was living and active. It was my pleasant privilege of knowing, as we Scotchmen would term it, "The Perry."

To me he was a man of great ideas, and deplorable it was that his words, coming from the mountains, did not always reach the seashore. The State of South Carolina never could boast of a more devoted son and hardly of a more clear-headed one. Whatever he said was open and true, without guile or after-thought, and what is more, he was calm and without passion. But he could not, nor can even God or law, conquer passion in others, and hence he was often misunderstood by the majority of his fellow-citizens, but only until then when they saw that he was right, and now they lament their short-sightedness. But with all this, the name of "Perry" goes out to the world more glorious. The eloquent counsellor of the State in his debates in the legislative halls, stood like a Cicero in argument with Cataline, and was always victorious in argument, even if the schemes of his adversaries prevailed, and afterwards redounded to their failure. This knowledge, however sad, redounds notwithstanding to the immortal glory of our lamented deceased and makes him immortal; therefore in his demise he is not lost to us nor lost to you, madam. He is living still amongst us, and in his sons, who walk in his ways and follow the counsel of their father, he is living forth. Let us revere and cherish his memory, as he has done well for us all; and let us now try to understand his counsel and emulate his virtues.

Thanking you again, my dear madam, permit me to subscribe myself.　　　　Your most obedient servant,

JOHN ALEXANDER.

(From Judge W. B. Reese.)

VANDERBILT UNIVERSITY,
NASHVILLE, TENN., July 20, 1889.

Mrs. B. F. Perry:

MY DEAR MADAM: I am exceedingly obliged to you for sending me the Biographical Sketches by Governor Perry, of South Carolina. I have not written my acknowledgments before because I wished *thoroughly* to read and study its contents. I have now done this and am able to say, with great confidence, that by its publication you have not only contributed one of the most interesting volumes lately published, but one containing much new and valuable information not elsewhere to be found.

Again thanking you, I am　　Very truly your obliged,

W. B. REESE.

"MINDFUL NOT OF HIMSELF."

COLUMBIA; RECTORY, Dec. 3d, 1889.

My Dear Mrs. Perry:

You would have heard from me before this, but I have been
so much engaged at home, and so unwell last week, I have not
had time to overlook the Phœnix for you.

I have now carefully overlooked the file, giving several
hours to it, and send you the references. Some of the matter
you have already published, but some of it has never been
printed.

And now, my dear and valued friend, I want to call your
attention to a reflection which your letter suggested to my
mind, which may be of comfort to you when you review the
political trials through which Governor Perry passed. Those
very trials and *bitter persecutions* you refer to, brought out
into prominence those traits of Governor Perry's *character*
which commanded the respect and admiration of his fellow-
citizens. They were bitter trials to him, but they furnished
him the opportunities for the display of those mental and
moral traits which stamped him before his friends and his
foes as a man of courage, faithfulness and unshaken heroism.
All this was fully appreciated by his people at the last, and if
he had not had the ordeal of his early life to demonstrate the
force of his character and his manly devotion to his convictions, his people would never have realized what a *man* he
was! The consciousness of his own integrity and his own sincerity, was an unfailing spring of both comfort and strength
to him through it all; a shield which turned and blunted the
shafts of detraction which would have pierced and wounded
and crushed a mere politician. In the article in The Phœnix,
September 15, nominating him for the U. S. Senate, among
other things said in his praise, are these words: "Let him receive the reward due his merit, loftiness of *character, integrity
of purpose* and enlightened wisdom." Remember, then, my
dear friend, that he passed through the fires to show all this;
and your comfort is, that trying as the passage was to him
and to you, he was greater than his trials, and came off with
honor to himself and the ultimate well-done of his people.

I send you herewith the notes I took from the files of the
paper in Mr. Calvo's office. You might write to Mr. Calvo

about the copying. It will take more time than I can command, or I would gladly oblige you and make the copies for you.

With much love to Fanny and Emily, I am, my dear Mrs. Perry,   Most truly yours,

E. CAPERS.

[*From the Files of The Phœnix.*]

Date—July 8, 1865.—Editorial on W. W. Boyce and B. F. Perry, both being nominated for Provisional Governor. Perry preferred and his fitness shown by an analysis of his character and past career.

July 22d.—Speech in Greenville.

"   "   Editorial on speech, *highly* in its praise.

Aug. 9th.—Long correspondence from a Cincinnati paper, from Washington, on the speech.

Aug. 15th.—Speech in Greenville on his return from Washington.

Aug. 17th.—Proclamation assuming the office of Governor.

Aug. 18th.—Order of General Gilmore respecting the same.

Sept. 6th.—Letter of W. H. Trescot to Governor Perry. Very interesting, giving report of his investigation of the subject of lands abandoned on the coast, etc. This is copied in The Phœnix from The Greenville Mountaineer.

Sept. 15th.—Article nominating Governor Perry for the U. S. Senate.

Sept. 15th.—Message No. 1 to the Convention.

Sept. 19th.—Proclamation of Governor Perry.

Sept. 28th.—Message No. 2 to Convention.

Oct. 19th.—Correspondence between Governor Perry and Seward, on the subject of the duration of his office as Provisional Governor.

Oct. 27th.—Message to the extra Legislature.

"   "   Editorial on the message.

28th.—What the South needs. An editorial on this theme, quoting largely from the Message.

Nov. 16th.—Correspondence between Secretary Seward and Governor Perry, communicated to the Legislature by Message.

Nov. 29th.—Message to Legislature.
" 30th.—Speech before the Legislature.
Dec. 3d.—Proclamation of Governor Perry.
Jan'y 2d, 1866.—Note of Governor Perry to The Phœnix, sending telegram of Secretary Seward terminating his office as Provisional Governor.

A perusal of the file of the paper shows The Phœnix to have been a *most appreciative* friend of Governor Perry's administration, and a *warm admirer* of the *man.*

E. C.

(From Judge B. C. Pressley.)

SUMMERVILLE, S. C., Dec. 23, 1889.

Mrs. B. F. Perry, Sans Souci:

DEAR MADAM: Miss Mittie Marshall kindly handed me on Saturday the beautiful copy of the Reminiscences, etc.,—your highly valued gift. I found it so absorbing that I almost finished it before the Lord's-day hour crept on me. Happy he who gave so much of his life to his native State, and yet found time to embalm the memory of so many of his valued friends. Happier yet in leaving a survivor who so long shared his inmost heart yearnings, to complete and make immortal his life work.

But is there no mistake in the seeming admission that his State did not properly appreciate and honor him? Strong convictions led him to cast his lot with the minority party, and hence the majority did not exalt him to high office; but if any ever failed to recognize his sincerity, splendid talents and unparallelled moral courage, they have never so said.

Please accept thanks for the volume. I value it greatly.

Very truly yours,
B. C. PRESSLEY.

(From Judge William H. Wallace.)

UNION, S. C., 27th Dec., 1889.

Mrs. B. F. Perry:

MY DEAR MADAM: I have delayed thanking you for a copy of Reminiscences with Speeches and Addresses by B. F. Perry,

Governor, etc., until I had had an opportunity to read the volume. I have read it with great pleasure. Besides the interesting sketches of public men and the eloquent and instructive speeches and addresses, the historical parts of the book relate to events in the history of the State that will always possess a deep interest for all the people of the State. In this history the author was a conspicuous actor, and this book permitting a glimpse of his whole public career, presents him in a most attractive point of view. In the great political struggle of 1832, he stood firmly by his convictions. Again in 1860 he gallantly led the forlorn hope of opposition to secession. He did all this in the face of overwhelming odds, and in opposition to numerous personal friends. When the State actually seceded and placed herself in a most perilous position while believing her action unwise; he claimed his place, as her son, by her side, to defend her rights and share her lot. Throughout these periods of political excitement he displayed a constancy, a courage and fidelity to conviction which proved the elevation of his character, and, when the excitement had subsided, won for him a noble eminence and crowned his latter years with honor and great offices, and the respect and admiration of troops of friends.

The loyalty of wifely affection, in giving these memorials to the public, has rendered an incalculable service to the State in preserving as a perpetual example and inspiration so great a character and so noble a career.

I am, very respectfully and sincerely,

Your obedient servant,
W. H. WALLACE.

CUSTOM-HOUSE, NEW ORLEANS, LA., }
SURVEYOR'S OFFICE, Dec. 17, 1889. }

Mrs. B. F. Perry, Greenville, S. C.:

DEAR MADAM: After reading the works of your lamented husband I realize, more fully than ever before what a happy combination there was in him of those high and noble qualities of head and heart that made him the patriot, philosopher and statesman. The youth of Carolina possess no richer

legacy than the life and example of such a man and your devotion to his memory does honor to Southern womanhood.

Respectfully, &c.,   JOHN C. VANCE.

(From Rev. A. Coke Smith.)

WOFFORD COLLEGE, ⎫
SPARTANBURG, Jan. 2, 1890. ⎭

Mrs. B. F. Perry, Greenville, S. C.:

DEAR MADAM: I acknowledge with hearty thanks the receipt this day of three volumes which you kindly sent me:
"Biographical Sketches" and "Reminiscences and Addresses"
by Governor Perry; and the memorial volume which your
love has prompted you to prepare from the many tributes
paid to the memory of your loved and greatly honored husband. It was my privilege to know Governor Perry personally, while I was pastor of the Buncombe-street Methodist
Church, in Greenville, and I hold his memory in deepest rev-
erence. Among my earliest recollections of the names of
South Carolina's leading men is that of your husband. My
father was a great admirer of him and they held the same
political views, so that Governor Perry was often quoted.

His life and labors as a public man have been a benefaction
to his State and to the country; and his pure and simple life
amidst the honors so generously bestowed upon him by our
admiring people, is at once an inspiration to the young men
to adhere to American simplicity and purity, and a rebuke to
the ostentatious display which is appearing in some parts of
our country.

Begging you to accept my thanks for your thoughtful kindness, and with assurances of highest esteem, I am, my dear
madam,   Yours with great respect,

A. COKE SMITH.

ALABAMA POLYTECHNIC INSTITUTE, ⎫
AUBURN, LEE CO., ALA., January 10, 1890. ⎭

Mrs. B. F. Perry, Greenville, S. C.,

MY DEAR MADAM: You will please accept my sincere thanks
for the Sketches, Addresses, &c., by your gifted husband, the

late Gov. B. F. Perry, you were so kind to send me. I appreciate most sensibly the favor.

The name of Gov. Perry has been familiar to me from my boyhood, and have often heard my uncles, who were residents of old Pendleton District, speak of him, especially my uncle, Colonel George Reese, who was his devoted political friend and admirer in the stormy days of nullification in South Carolina.

My father, the late Dr. David A. Reese, who at one time represented the Seventh Georgia Congressinal District, had a high opinion of Governor Perry, as a man of undaunted courage, unwavering and unflinching in all that he thought was right, in all questions affecting the interest and welfare of the South and the whole country.

The death of such a man as your husband, though at a ripe old age, was lamentable. Few men in this day and time of action displayed such moral courage, or possessed such sound and conservative views from any standpoint.

His memory will be the more cherished as the years go by, and his virtues and great worth as a patriot and statesman will be the more admired and lustrous.

Wishing you many years of happiness in your beautiful and charming home, Sans Souci, which my young and lovely friend, Miss Minnie Armstrong, of this place, has so graphically described. I am sincerely yours,

FRANK M. REESE.

BIRMINGHAM, January 5, 1890.

MY DEAR MRS. PERRY: Absence from my desk must be my apology for a delayed acknowledgment of your repeated kindness in sending to me the "Tribute to the Memory of Benjamin Franklin Perry." I sincerely thank you. I enclose herewith a leading editorial from the Birmingham Chronicle, which I wrote, although I am not on the staff of the paper. I have found the writings of Governor Perry indispensable to my intelligence and most comforting to my hopes of my country. I have read and re-read them, and always take them up with awakened expectations and lay them down when I am forced to go on with the labor which daily bread exacts.

Mr. B. C. Yancey, not knowing that I had been the recipient of your favor, took the trouble to send me the volumes you had given him as a loan, charging me to return them promptly when I had read them. So you see your old friends, and your illustrious husband's friends, are yet true.

Mr. Yancey said in his letter: "I send the books received as a present from Mrs. Perry, a friend of fifty years."

Since I last wrote to you my father died in his 81st year. Perhaps I sent you a newspaper notice of his life and death. He was an inveterate reader all last summer, and up to the week which was his last, of the things written by Governor Perry of South Carolina.

I hope the New Year finds you well, and beg to remain,
Very truly your friend,
JOHN W. DuBOSE.

(*From the Birmingham Evening Chronicle, Jan. 2, 1890.*)

A NOBLE MONUMENT.—The Chronicle is pleased to peruse the several volumes, published by Mrs. Benjamin Franklin Perry, of South Carolina, of the writings of her late illustrious husband. It seems that from early manhood Governor Perry practiced the pleasing pastime of writing down his observations at the time of living men and current events. At the age of eighty-one, when he died, a great mass of manuscript carefully stored in his large library was found by his wife. The volumes to which we refer are the publication in convenient and handsome book style of some of these writings. They are a reliable compendium of the great events of forty to fifty years. The style is fascinating in its simplicity, and captivating are the useful lessons its pages teach. Almost every great man of America was known personally to Governor Perry, and it is of such men and their every day life he wrote. Calhoun was his neighbor, Lieber was his friend, Huger, Webster, Gen. Scott, Andrew Johnson, William L. Yancey and men great in every occupation, are here brought to the eye of posterity; not a few, but scores of them.

The volumes may be safely compared to Plutarch in beauty of style and reliability of history.

Mrs. Perry brings them forward with natural pride in their intrinsic merit, and in this most opportune manner erects a monument more lasting than brass to her distinguished husband. No man lived in South Carolina in these latter decades who commanded to a greater degree the universal confidence than Gov. B. F. Perry.

MAINE STATE COLLEGE OF AGRICULTURE AND MECHANIC ARTS,
ORONO, MAINE, January 7, 1890.

Mrs. B. F. Perry,

DEAR MADAM: I have read with very deep interest the tributes to the memory of your late lamented husband, and beg to thank you most sincerely for the little volume that you add to our college library.

It must be a source of great satisfaction to you to have so abundant evidence of the high appreciation and regard in which he was held by those who value the most exalted qualities of human nature.

In preserving in permanent form his valuable papers and the tributes of esteem which testify so fully to his worth, you are conferring a benefit upon your State and a lasting good upon the community at large who cannot fail to profit by so noble an example. I am, dear madam,

Yours very sincerely,

M. C. FERNALD, *President.*

U. S. GRANT UNIVERSITY, ATHENS AND CHATTANOOGA.
ATHENS, TENN., January 16, 1890.

Mrs. Governor B. F. Perry,

I beg to gratefully acknowledge the courtesy conferred by you in sending to our Library a copy "In Memoriam" of Benjamin Franklin Perry. Our students will highly prize the little volume; and it will doubtless be a real gem in the University Library.

I would gladly have the splendid character of your precious husband, with all its moral worth, firmness and courage, lithographed upon the mind and heart of every student within our halls. With great respect I am

Sincerely yours,

J. F. SPENCE,
Chancellor Grant University.

(From Rev. Richard D. Smart.)

CHARLESTON, S. C., January 17, 1890.

MRS. B. F. PERRY, *Greenville, S. C.:*

MY DEAR MRS. PERRY: From my heart I thank you for your continued and kind remembrance of me. I am glad that you have preserved the "Sketches" and the "Reminiscences" of your distinguished husband for the benefit of the present and the succeeding generations. A copy of each was received in excellent condition.

At such a time as this it seems that we are *specially* in need of men like Governor Perry. The noble example left by him is a rich legacy to those who come after him.

Assuring you of my sincere regard, and praying that He who is the Father of the fatherless and the widow's God may provide for you in your necessities, and comfort you in your sorrows, I remain,

Faithfully your friend,

R. D. SMART.

(From Judge Oliver Miller, Judge of the Supreme Court of Maryland.)

ANNAPOLIS, Dec. 25th, 1889.

DEAR MADAM: I write this Christmas day to acknowledge the receipt of the works and tributes to the memory of Governor Perry—your deceased husband. I am reading them with great interest and pleasure. I remember him well and have had his portrait framed and hanging in my office since his visit here, with yourself, many years ago to place his son Frank in the Naval Academy. On that occasion I was glad to do your son some slight service; but alas! the physicians at the Academy were right in regard to the state of his health. That was long ago, and since we have all encountered affliction and distress from the terrible war.

The Governor was a man I always admired, and he deserves all that is so well said of him in these books. If there had been *more* such men, the recent history of the country would have been far different. At all events *his* fame and reputation are *secure*.

Very truly yours,

OLIVER MILLER.

Mrs. Governor B. F. Perry, Greenville, S. C.

VANDERBILT BENEVOLENT ASSOCIATION,
A. C. KAUFMAN, President.

CHARLESTON, S. C., March 24, 1890.

MY DEAR MADAM: I feel obligated to you, as must, indeed, any one who has been similarly honored, at your thoughtful gift embraced in the valuable Memoirs to your patriot husband.

It is said that early impressions are the most lasting. My first recollection of Gov. Perry dates back to my youth in 1860, when, as a member of the National Democratic Convention, assembled in Charleston, he then exhibited those traits of mind that fixed him in my mind as a man of Roman mould. From that time on did I watch his career most closely, with all his acts to admire and nothing to condemn.

Those who are familiar with the history of the three past decades, remember. as a part of that history, the men who achieved greatness during that period, especially in the early part of the decade beginning in 1860. No nobler name is inscribed therein than that of "Benjamin Franklin Perry," of whom it may honestly be said that for his country he lived; and died, leaving her his blessing behind him.

These Memoirs will be placed among the archives of this Association and be sacredly treasured by its members as a precious legacy for all time to come.

No books that I have ever read possess the fascination that meets one at every step in these Memorial volumes. They do credit to the head and heart of both author and compiler. Every time these books are opened some new charm appears, and their pages seem invested with fresh beauty. and Immortality to "Benjamin Franklin Perry,"—hero, patriot, sage, *almost* MARTYR, yet in the end victor—the grand old gentleman!

To his faithful wife in her declining years, serenity and joy; "and may the peace of God, which passeth all understanding, keep her heart and mind."

With great respect, I am, my dear madam,

    Your friend and servant,   A. C. KAUFMAN.

To Mrs. B. F. Perry, Greenville, S. C.

UNION, S. C., March 14th, 1890.

MRS. B. F. PERRY, *Greenville, S. C.:*

MY DDAR MADAM: Your kind letter of a few days ago has been received, and I hasten to thank you for your very great kindness in remembering me in the friendly distribution of your reminiscences of your noble husband.

I cannot express to you my great appreciation of your kindness. I am sure I have no books that I shall cherish with stronger devotion and tenderer care than those you have been so kind as to send to me. In my humble estimation —and I am yet a mere youth—there has been no man, since the establishment of this Republic, who combined more of the very noblest qualities of pure statesmanship than your husband. In all his public speeches and writings can be easily detected those characteristics that make up the sum total of pure statesmanship, pure manhood and nobility of heart; and in all those utterences the student of history shall find his most valuable assistance in discerning what nobility of heart and greatness of character was found at all times in the personality of Governor B. F. Perry. It was my pleasure to touch his garment and grasp his hand only once; but from him I have learned what it is to command the applause of listening senates and defy the vituperation of opposing demagogues.

I am sure you are now doing a noble work, and I am equally confident that your devotion and love for your dead husband has never been equalled in the history of modern times. I hope to see you soon and then I can thank you personally for the books.

With great esteem, I am,

Very truly, your friend always,

E. P. McKISSICK.

WAVERLY, NEAR WHITE POST, VA.,
17th March, 1890.

MRS. B. F. PERRY, *Greenville, S. C.:*

MY DEAR MADAM: Honestly, I am at a loss for words with which to express my deep sense of gratitude and high appreciation of your kindness in sending me the valuable present, "Reminiscences by Governor Perry," (second series.) It is enough for me to say that I feel profoundly grateful and thank you, my dear madam, most sincerely for it.

I have now, I presume, the only volumes incident to the life and history of your honored husband, two having been previously sent me by my friend and your son, Doctor Perry. It is needless for me to say how very, *very* highly I value them. They were at once taken possession of and claimed by my daughter, Fannie, the only book-worm of the family, and who insisted upon having her name written in them. I will take the liberty of lending the books to some of my lawyer friends of Winchester, Benyville and Front Royal, which may be the means of having some copies sold.

As I stated in one of my letters to the doctor, the name of Governor Perry was not only perfectly familiar to me, but has been—to me—for many years as "a household word." I recall, distinctly, his herculean efforts in behalf of the Union in his own State, which even to us, in Virginia, who entertained the same views which he and our own great man, Henry A. Wise, did, viz., that our policy was to fight for our rights *in* the Union and not *out* of it, as words of comfort, wisdom and strength. Governor Perry was a great and *good* man, and the world was that much better that he lived in it. No greater compliment could be paid any one. It is useless now to repine that *his* words of warning and wisdom, together with those of his associate patriots, *for* the Union were not heeded. That is all past, forever gone, and we have to make the best we can of it. They tell us it was all for the best, and that future generations will derive the benefits of our new order of things. That may be all true—I do not say that it isn't—but, for my part, I am free to admit that I would have greatly preferred that they *deferred* their change until I had passed from the scene of action. You and I, my dear Mrs. Perry, are rather too old for the ups and downs of life to sit easily upon our shoulders, it matters not how gracefully we may endeavor to bear them.

Yes, I repeat, that I distinctly recall the memory of your pure and excellent husband; and, with unaffected feelings, hang before it my small chaplet of immortelles.

Should I go to Washington before the adjournment of Congress, I shall most assuredly do myself the honor of making the acquaintance of your distinguished son.

Please present me most kindly to the doctor, and believe me, my dear madam, sincerely, your friend,

WM. C. KENNERLY.

UNIVERSITY OF SOUTH CAROLINA,

COLUMBIA, S. C., March 22, 1890.

MRS. B. F. PERRY, *Greenville, S. C.*:

MY DEAR MADAM: I feel honored to be thought worthy to receive at your hands the inestimable memorials of your illustrious husband, compiled and published by your loving care. They constitute not only a monument to himself and to you and a priceless heritage to his descendants, but they are a noble legacy to his State and country. I wish that all the young men of South Carolina could be brought to study and emulate the solid virtues so nobly exhibited in the life and character of Governor Perry.

I am, dear madam, with high regard,

Yours very truly,

EDWARD S. JOYNES.

BRIEF SKETCH

OF THE

LIFE AND MILITARY SERVICES OF ARTHUR P. HAYNE,

OF CHARLESTON, S. C.

(PUBLISHED IN PHILADELPHIA IN 1837—AUTHOR UNKNOWN.)

This Sketch of my uncle, Colonel Arthur P. Hayne is out of print. He was a good man—my mother's brother—and the sketch will prove he was a distinguished United States Army officer, the intimate friend of General Andrew Jackson. I deem it worthy of preservation for this and future generations, and embrace the opportunity to place it in this book dedicated to my husband, peculiarly appropriate, as they entertained for each other a mutual esteem and admiration. MRS. B. F. PERRY.

It is but too common to transfer to the commanding officers, all the merit of military exploits, and to yield to the General exclusively the meed of gratitude and praise, which belongs at least equally to the army. Every well informed man knows how much the success of the greatest commanders has depended upon the character of their officers, and yet in our anxiety to do homage to military glory, we usually yield all our admiration to the chief, and "crown the *victor with laurels*," without bestowing even a thought upon those who have been the instruments of his renown. In every well organised army, there is a class of officers who constitute its chief strength; who organize, and arrange everything, and carry into effect the plans of the commander in chief. They are the eyes through which he sees, the ears through which he hears, the arms by which he subdues the foe. It is the highest attribute of a great General, to have the faculty of discerning merit, and the ability of using all the means at his disposal in the best manner for the accomplishment of his ends. Washington possessed this rare quality in a high degree, and General Andrew Jackson showed throughout his campaigns that he knew both how to select and how to use the best talent of his army, to effect his purposes. It is equally due to this officer to add, that he never failed to acknowledge his obligations to those of his subalterns who contributed to his success. He did them ample justice on all occasions, and loved to honour and advance them.

It is our present purpose to afford an illustration of the truth of these remarks, by giving a short biographical sketch of a distinguished officer of the late war, whose rank did not permit him to command an army, but whose conduct contributed, in an eminent degree, to the success of our arms, and whose services entitle him to a large share of the public gratitude. Our materials have been drawn from the best sources, and we shall give documents which will speak for themselves.

Col. Arthur P. Hayne, the subject of this sketch, was born in Charleston, South Carolina, on the 12th day of March, 1790, of a respectable *Whig stock* distinguished in the Revolution by their services and sacrifices. His grandfather by the paternal line died of a fever contracted on board a British prison ship, and his near relation, Colonel Isaac Hayne, expired on the scaffold, a martyr to the liberty of his country. Having recieved a good education, he determined to become a merchant, and remained four years in a counting house, where he was distinguished for correct conduct, diligence and intelligence. When the attack was made on the frigate Chesapeake in 1807, although not of age, partaking of the enthusiasm which spread through the whole country, he came at once to the resolution to enter the army, and accordingly obtained a commission as first lieutenant in the regiment of light dragoons, which was commanded by that distinguished soldier of the revolution, Colonel Wade Hampton. In 1809, he was ordered by General Hampton to the Mississippi, the only place at that time in our country, where a respectable military force was concentrated, and there with Covington, Pike, Scott, and Gaines, holding the same rank as the two latter, the foundation of his military knowledge was laid, and he was prepared for future usefulness in the profession of his choice. In 1812, war having been declared, he was

ordered by the government to the north, and soon after his
arrival there, we find him engaged in the battle and victory
of Sackett's Harbour—a victory in which *seven hundred* regulars, under the command of that veteran soldier, Lieutenant Colonel Backus, (who there received a mortal wound
through his breast,) and about *one hundred and fifty* volunteers, aided by a few militia, all under the command of Brigadier General Brown, beat back *fifteen hundred* regulars,
commanded by Sir George Prevost, who was supported by
the enemy's fleet, under the command of Sir James Yeo. In
consideration of the services he rendered in this battle Captain Hayne was promoted to the command of a squadron of
cavalry, with the rank of a Major in the line of the army.
He accompanied General Wilkinson down the St. Lawrence,
in the campaign of 1813, in the contemplated attack on
Montreal. In his division of the army, General Hampton
ton was particularly anxious to have *Hayne* and *Haig,* and
in a letter to General Armstrong, Secretary of war, are these
complimentary expressions—to wit: *"Send me Hayne and
Haig; I want their constitutional ardour—it will add much
to the strength of my army."*

It was not the fortune of Hayne to be in the battle of
Chrystler's Fields, where the first rate soldier, Colonel Cum-
ming of Georgia, so greatly distinguished himself, and that
too, after having received a ball through the *thigh.* On this occasion Major Hayne was attached to the advanced corps of
the army, under Brigadier General Brown, about twenty
miles in van of the main body. This corps was engaged often
with the enemy, and was always victorious.

Early in 1814, that peculiarly gifted and highly talented
officer, General Jackson, was brought into the regular army,
and at the same time Major Hayne received from General
Armstrong, the Secretary of war, the important appointment of Inspector General, and was forthwith ordered to
join Jackson in the Creek nation. After the ratification of
the treaty of Fort Jackson, Colonel Hayne, in August, 1814,
accompanied General Jackson to Mobile, descending the river
Alabama, and that excellent officer, Colonel Butler, the
Adjutant General, having been dispatched to Tennessee on

military business, Colonel Hayne was called upon to act in double capacity of Adjutant General. and Inspector General to the army. Early in the autumn of 1814, Jackson, having determined to drive the enemy from Pensacola, directed Colonel Hayne to proceed to Fort Montgomery, the point upon which the army was to concentrate, having invested him with the necessary authority to organize the forces, preparatory to the movement upon Florida.

At the storming of Pensacola, which was achieved on the 7th of November, 1814. the gallant Mayor W. Laval, of Charleston, South Carolina, (who there recieved a most severe wound,) with Colonel Hayne, was among the *very first* who siezed possession of the enemy's battery, amidst a most destructive fire from the houses occupied by the enemy, on both sides of the streets, as well as from the Spanish battery directly in front. As General Jackson was proceeding against Fort Barancas, which is some distance below Pensacola, and the British troops remained on board their shipping, he entrusted the safety of the city to Hayne, with about five hundred men. So soon as the enemy's fleet had left the harbour, as General Jackson was compelled to visit Mobile, he directed Colonel Hayne to advance with all possible rapidity to New Orleanes, and immediately on his arrival to repair without delay to the mouth of the Mississippi, and there to " *examine and determine*, whether a fortification at the Balize, near the bar, would give greater security to New Orleans." After a rapid movement he reached New Orleans, and instantly repaired to the designated spot, when, upon full examination he was satisfied that no advantage would result from its being fortified, and in his official report pronounced Fort St. Philip the *key* of all of our positions upon the Mississippi; all of which opinions and views General Jackson approved and confirmed. It was from Fort St. Philip, it will be recollected, that Major Overton in so skillful a manner repelled a part of the British fleet.

In the attack on the British army, on the night of the 23d December, 1814, Colonel Hayne was eminently conspicuous, and it has even been considered that the brilliant result of this daring measure was the saving of New Orleans. On this occasion, so eventful, so soon as General Jackson understood that the enemy had landed in considerable force a short distance below the city, he despatched Colonel Hayne with five hundred men, composed of Major Hinds' squadron of dragoons from the State of Mississippi, the Orleans rifle corps, commanded by Captain Beal, and a company of mounted gunmen, with orders to proceed forthwith against the enemy, to reconnoitre his position, ascertain his strength, and, were they found advancing, to harass them at every step, until the main body of our army should be concentrated, and prepared for defence. These high duties were executed with equal faithfulness and promptitude, and with the loss of but a single man. Colonel Hayne estimated the enemy at *two thousand*; they have since been ascertained to have been about *three thousand*. "The result of this victory," says an authentic account, "was the saving of New Orleans. The pride of an arrogant foe was humbled the first moment that he presumed to profane the soil of freedom by his hostile tread. It produced confidence in our ranks, established unanimity, and at once crushed disaffection. The *"ensemble"* of the general movement, with its various combinations, was maintained and fully realized throughout the whole battle. It was not an exhibition of mere physical strength, as is too often the case, but in every stage of the battle, we clearly perceive the effects produced by the admirable arrangements of the commanding General: and like Cæsar, he, also, might have said, *" Veni, Vidi, Vici."* In his official communication to the Secretary of two of these masterly achievements, in which were exhibited the skill of Scipio, and the devotion of Curtius, General Jackson says: *" Colonel Hayne was every where that duty or danger called."*

There was another South Carolinian, who largely participated in the glories of New Orleans. We mean Colonel Wade Hampton, of Columbia, South Carolina. He had reached his father's plantation on the Mississippi, sixty miles above New Orleans, but a few days after the campaign had commenced, and, without a moment's delay, he hastened to the scene of battle, and enrolled himself *as a private soldier in the ranks of the army.* Patriotism so elevated, excited an admiration at that crisis peculiarly salutary, and could not escape an eye like Jackson's. The appointment of Acting Assistant Inspector General was immediately conferred on him, and he was attached to the department of his friend Hayne. In this situation, he eminently distinguished himself throughout the whole campaign, particularly on the 8th of January, and, at once, merited and received the repeated encomiums of the illustrious commander. In the *"General Orders,"* the manner in which this department was conducted is thus handsomely characterized by Jackson: "The skill, vigilance,. courage, and constant attention to duty exhibited during the campaign, by Colonel Hayne, and his two assistants, Majors Davis and Hampton, have been appreciated as they deserve to be, by the commanding General."

On the repulse of the British at New Orleans, it is well known, that, though peace had been made, this was not only unknown to General Jackson, but that officer was under the. impression that increased vigilance, and more extensive preparations had become necessary, to maintain the country which he had so successfully defended. Full of anxiety on this subject, he determined to send a confidential officer to Washington, to arrange with the government the measures to be adopted for this purpose. His choice fell upon Colonel Hayne, and he was accordingly despatched on this difficult and delicate duty, the bearer of the following interesting letter, the use of which we have obtained and it is annexed. It is a document which belongs to the history of the country, and is creditable to all parties concerned. It contains a merited tribute of respect to several officers, whose good deeds should be handed down to posterity, as an example to others, and as a legacy to their children.

———

"*Head Quarters, New Orleans, 25th January*, 1815.

"SIR:—It is my desire, when you arrive at Washington, that you would impress on the mind of the Secretary of War, the necessity of expediting regular troops to the defense of this district. General Coffee's brigade will be entitled to honourable discharge on the 20th of March—General Carroll's division about the 15th of May—and General Thomas's detachment from Kentucky about the same time. The present regular force does not exceed six hundred effectives.

"Prevented by motives of delicacy and other causes, I have not made those discriminations, nor urged those pretensions, which the respective merits of officers required. I must therefore request you to mention the names of Major Pierre, and Captains Butler and Baker of the 44th regiment, and of acting Lieutenant Call,* as worthy of promotion. Captains Montgomery, Vail and Allen of the 7th regiment, acting well during the whole campaign. They are certainly good captains, and merit promotion. Too much praise cannot be bestowed on Captain Humphrey, and Lieutenant Spotts of the Artillery—Humphrey ought to be at the head of a regiment, and the latter of a company. I cannot omit. to mention the names of the Adjutant General Colonel Robert Butler, and his Assistant Adjutant General Major Chotard, also the Assistant Inspector General Major Davis, and my too aids, Captains Reed and Butler. From the report of Major Overton, Captains Woolstonecraft, Murray and White, ought to be noticed, and the Major is worthy to command a regiment. The Brave defenders of Fort Bowyer have been too long neglected. Their gallantry at one moment saved that section of the country.

"From General Coffee's brigade, I am satisfied most valuable officers might be selected. The General would be a most valuable brigadier. Colonels Dyer, Elliot, and Gibson are men of the utmost bravery. Captain Parish would do honour to the head of a company in any army. Captain Martin would, I have no doubt, command a company well. The government, and the world are sensible of the high opinion I entertain of General Carroll. General Adair is certainly a valuable officer, and ought to be noticed. As a brigadier his superior is perhaps nowhere to be found. In General Coffee,s brigade, there are Captain Donaldson of the rangers, and Captain Hutchins of the mounted gunmen, whose names I have omitted asking you to mention, because they are my near connections.

"Any officers, whose merits you may have noticed, and no doubt there are many such, you will be good enough to do

*Now Governor of Florida.

justice to, and for God's sake entreat the Secretary of War, not to yield too much, in time to come, to recommendations of *members of Congress*. He must be sensible of the motives from which, for the most part, such recommendations proceed, and events have too often and too sadly proved how little merit they imply.

"To all matters connected with the welfare and defence of this district, you will have the goodness to direct the attention of the Secretary of War; and be assured, sir, when you are thus about to leave me at the close of a campaign, which has been so full of interest, and to the successful prosecution of which your skill, and courage, have so much contributed, I should do no less injustice to my own feelings, than to your merits, did I not return you my warmest acknowledgements. Be assured, sir, wherever you go, you carry with you my high sense of your services, my thanks for them, and my prayers for your prosperity. I am your friend,

(Signed)   "ANDREW JACKSON.

"Major General Commanding.

"For Col. ARTHUR P. HAYNE,

"Inspector General, Southern Division, &c., &c., New Orleans."

There is an anecdote connected with the battle of New Orleans, so honourable to Colonel Hayne, and so interesting in itself, that we cannot refrain from giving it here, having ascertained, from the highest source, its unquestionable authority. After the battle of the night of the 23d December, Colonel Hayne, having been on horseback from nine o'clock in the morning till twelve o'clock at night, requested the commanding general, while the troops were lying under arms, to allow him to proceed to his quarters in the city to take some refreshment. It was on his return to the field of battle, that he surveyed, with a military eye, the different positions which might be defended, so as to prevent the enemy from reaching the city, and selected the very spot for the purpose, which General Jackson subsequently approved at his suggestion, and where the enemy were so gloriously repulsed on the 8th of January.

Before we close the history of Colonel Hayne's military life,

during the late war with England, it it proper that we should
advert to one or two circumstances highly honorable to him;
and which may serve to shed some light on the military history of the country. At the battle of Sackett's Harbour,
"*the first of his fields*," it is known that the *brunt* fell upon
the 1st regiment of light dragoons, then acting as infantry,
under the immediate command of Lieutenant Colonel Backus.
General Brown, afterwards so much distinguished, (then a
Brigadier General in the New York militia,) was commander
in chief. That officer has often been heard to declare, that,
notwithstanding all the hard fighting, which he afterwards
witnessed on the northern frountier at Chippeway, Bridge-
water, the sortie from Fort Erie, and elsewhere, he never saw
more steadiness, or greater gallantry displayed by any troops,
than by the officers and men belonging to the regiment of
dragoons at Sackett's Harbour. We here annex the following letter written by General Brown's *order* to Colonel Hayne,
as valuable testimony to the gallantry of a noble band,
many of whom have indeed paid the debt of nature, but some
still survive, and we trust will long live in the affections of
a grateful country.

"HEAD QUARTERS, WASHINGTON CITY.
"*February* 11*th* 1828.
"SIR: I address you at the request of Major General
Brown, for the purpose of recalling to your mind a scene in
the late war in which you were both actors. I allude to the
battle of the 29th of May, 1813, at Sackett's Harbour. The
General is desirous of obtaining the names of a portion of
the brave men who fought on that occasion, and knows of no
one to whom he can apply with so much propriety as to
yourself. He considers the day to which I allude *as one of
the most interesting and important of his life, and he directs
me to say, that during .the whole course of his service, he
never witnessed a nobler display of determined valour, than
was exhibited on that occasion, on the part of the detachment of dragoons, who fought under the lamented Backus.*
It is the desire of the General to perpetrate the names of the
chivalric officers of that little band, that induces him to

make the present application to you, and in so doing, he is happy in having it in his power to express to one of those officers, his admiration of the devotedness they exhibited, for the honour of their country. You will no doubt be able to communicate the names of most of your comrades, who were with you on the 29th of May, 1813, as well as to specify the part of the country from which they came, with many other interesting particulars of the action which fell under your immediate notice.

"The General will leave behind him particulars of some of the most interesting periods of his life, and he hopes that his account of the events at Sackett's Harbour will be much enriched by the information you will communicate.

"He directs me to assure you of his great respect and esteem.

" I have the honor to be, sir, very repectfully your most obedient servant.   (Signed)   J. S. BROWN,
                                                          "Aid de Camp.

" For Colonel ARTHUR P. HAYNE,
    "Late Adjutant General Northern Division of the U. S. Army."

We should have before observed that Colonel Hayne was brevetted at Sackett's Harbour—indeed he was brevetted for gallant conduct no less than three times during the war, a circumstance which speaks volumes in his praise, viz: Frst for his services at Sackett's Harbour; next for his services at the storming of Pensacola, and lastly, for his services at the battle of the night of the 23d December, and at the siege of New Orleans.

The war with England concluded, Colonel Hayne determined to devote himself to the pursuits of private life, and therefore returned his militaty commission to the government; but, contrary to his expectations or even wishes, he was retained in the army as Adjutant General to the northern division, the Inspector Generalship having been abolished under the new organization. This honourable appointment he accepted, upon the condition he should be indulged with a furlough to prosecute legal studies, to which the gov-

ernment assented; and having completed the usual course
under the direction of that distinguished civilian, the late
Judge Duncan, his friend and near connection, his father-in-
law, he was admitted to the bar of Pennsylvania.   About this
period the army was organized anew, the inspector's department restored, and, at the particular request of General
Jackson, Colonel Hayne was transferred again to this office,
and attached to his division.

During the second Florida campaign, he was placed by
General Jackson, at the head of the Tennessee volunteers,
with full authority to organize a brigade staff, and also
every power necessary to facilitate their movement to the
scene of action.   The Secretary of War, Mr. Calhoun, speaking of the manner in which Colonel Hayne had acquitted
himself on this occasion, uses these expressions: "I am well
aware of the difficulties to be overcome to organize efficient-
ly, and with satisfaction to the officers and men, a volun-
teer corps for the field.   In the present instance, the pride
and spirits of veterans, aided by patriotism, and directed by
superior intelligence, have handsomely surmounted every
obstacle."

In 1820, Colonel Hayne, after services highly beneficial to
our country, and honourable to himself, retired from the
army, and General Jackson, in his communication to the
war department, repeats the flattering opinion of one, whose
merits he possessed every opportunity correctly to estimate.

"It is due," says he, "to Colonel Hayne, to express my
approbation of his conduct, during his long connection with
my military family, and warmly to recommend him to the
notice of the government as a soldier of high sense of honour, great worth, and intelligence."

With this tribute to the merit of Colonel Hayne, in the exalted estimation of his character by General Jackson, we
turn from his military history, and follow him into the walks
of private life.   On his return home, Colonel Hayne was received by his fellow citizens with the respect and affection due
to his high character and distinguished services; and he had
hardly settled among them, before the citizens of Charleston
required his services in the state legislature, where he con-

tinued to serve with great credit to himself, until he went to
Europe in the important and highly responsible station of
Agent for Naval Affairs in the Mediterranean, in which capacity he served honourably and most acceptably to the
navy for nearly five years.

On the return of the Honourable Hugh S. Legare, late minister to the court at Belgium, to the United States, the President tendered to Colonel Hayne that foreign mission, which
he declined accepting, as, from the smallness of the salary, it
might envolve him in pecuniary embarrassment. The fact
is, our ministers abroad are very inadequately paid, and unless their private resources are most ample, they generally
return home in debt for the balance of their lives. This
ought not to be the case, and is a great evil, which calls for
prompt redress. There is, however, one exception, and that
is, the mission to France.

Of his services in the legislature we have been assured, by a
distinguished gentleman,* who served with him in the legislature, "that Colonel Hayne's frank and gentlemanly de-
portment, elevated principles, and ardent character, soon
developed themselves in the legislature, and he became a
prominent and efficient member on the floor. He was ap-
pointed Chairman of the military committee, and made a most
sensible report on the military organization of the state.
At the first session, Colonel Hayne was elected by joint ballot of both houses of the legislature, an elector (on the part
of the State) of President and Vice-President of the United
States. This early selection of Colonel Hayne, as an elector,
was equally honourable and flattering to him, as it afforded
him the opportunity of bearing his public testimony to the
private worth and public services of his patron and brother
soldier, the hero of New Orleans."

Another of his colleagues,‡ equally distinguished for talents, says: "Although not accustomed to extemporaneous
debate, yet Colonel Hayne's clear conceptions and correct
opinions always found a ready, dignified and manly utter-
ance, and upon occasions requiring previous preparations,

*Henry A. DesSaussure, Esquire.
‡Honourable James Gregg.

his energetic, glowing and lofty manner was exceedingly commanding and eloquent. But that which constituted Colonel Hayne's chief superiority, and rendered his services during his legislative career invaluable, was his liberal, enlarged, and elevated mind, which was calculated to give tone and character to the house, and which never failed to diffuse through the entire body, of which he was a member, those noble and exalted feelings and sentiments, which have always distinguished the legislature of South Carolina. He seemed never to forget he was legislating for the country, which had been enlightened by the Pinckney's and Rutledges; and conforming his course to the *models* formed by those illustrious patriots and statesmen, he contributed his full share to preserve and perpetuate in the councils of his native State that elevated character, which those departed sages had been so instrumental in establishing."

In concluding this brief and imperfect sketch of this gentleman, we will only add, that Colonel Hayne has been distinguished through life, for high honour, chivalric courage, courteous manners, and the most exemplary discharge of his duties, in all the private relations of life. As the soldier—the citizen—the man—he is a fair specimen of a Southern gentleman of the best school.

At the meeting of the Bar at Abbeville, expressing their appreciation of Judge A. P. Aldrich's character, W. C. Benet, Esq., said:

"This State owes a debt of gratitude to the venerable widow of the late Governor Perry for publishing his 'Reminiscences, with Speeches and Addresses.' No more valuable work has been published in South Carolina during a quarter of a century. Its biographical sketches of Governor Perry's contemporaries—judges, lawyers, governors and public men—have rescued from inconstant, untrustworthy tradition, if not from oblivion, the memory of many distinguished men. Governor Perry discharged his debt to his day and generation."

CPSIA information can be obtained
at www.ICGtesting.com
Printed in the USA
BVOW06s1113131017
497599BV00020B/791/P